Winning Big
In HR

**100+ Powerful Strategies For
Accomplishing Great Results Faster
& Getting Your Clients To Rave About You
As A Human Resources Professional!**

Alan Collins

Success in HR Publishing
Chicago, Illinois USA

Dedicated to my son, Bryan.

Fifty percent of the proceeds of this book will
go to the Bryan A. Collins Memorial Scholarship Program
which provides scholarships to deserving, high potential
minority students who excel in academics and in
service to others. I encourage you to join me in
supporting this truly worthwhile cause at
www.BryanCollinsScholarship.org.

CONTENTS

HR Career Success Resources
by Alan Collins

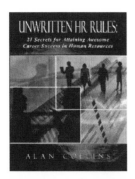

How To Gain The Most Value From This Book!

In *Winning Big in HR*, you have in your hands the most powerful strategies for achieving great results faster and getting your clients rave about you as a Human Resources professional.

This book has an amazing collection of over 100 of the best pieces of career advice, compelling stories and insights stolen from my blog, *SuccessInHR.com* -- along with some brand new strategies I've never shared.

If you're a busy, overworked HR professional who doesn't have time to read a book from cover to cover, this has been written especially for you.

To get the biggest bang for the buck from these pages...

#1: Use it as an "energy boost" for your own performance and HR career. Use it to provide a jolt of inspiration or a whack on the rump when you need it. Some of this you will want to move on immediately. Some of this you'll want to digest first, before acting. It's not practical to attempt to put all these insights into action at

once. You'll go crazy. So, take one idea at a time and use it. Then go to another page, swipe another nugget from there and apply it. Or take out the highlighter, mark up the pages or even put big x's through those things that you don't agree with. The key is to make this yours.

#2: Have it available to you at all times as your own private, portable coach. Carry it with

you when you travel. Have it on your nightstand. Keep it on your desk. Have it available in the john as bathroom reading. Often, when you least expect it, you'll get a brand new and empowering perspective while scanning through the strategies, stories and tips. Let this book provide you with the advice and insight you need, exactly when you need it.

#3: Share this with your HR staff. If you're an

HR leader and need your team to play a bigger game, pass a copy of this book on to them as part of their development. Encourage them to try out or discuss or debate these insights with you. Ask them what they agree with and what they don't. Find out what parts of this book inspires or upsets them. Either way, I'm sure you and they will be positively enriched from the discussion and the experience.

Thank you in advance for investing your time in this book. I hope you enjoy it.

--*Alan Collins*

Now let's get started!

Step Up!

Take Charge & Seize Opportunities!

This is where it all starts. To get **<u>GREAT</u> <u>RESULTS</u> <u>FAST</u>**, you must step up. Stepping up is seeing a need in Human Resources and then deciding YOU are the right person to do something about it.

It is NOT finger-pointing.

It is NOT passing the buck.

It is NOT blaming the CEO.

It is NOT blaming your boss.

It is NOT blaming your clients.

It is NOT blaming your team members.

It is NOT blaming "the culture."

It is NOT whining because no one else will step up.

It is NOT waiting on someone to tell you what to do.

It is DOING what you can within <u>YOUR</u> own sphere of influence to take charge, gain support, make things happen and <u>NOT</u> LOOKING TO ANYONE ELSE.

Don't Wait for Direction, Provide It!

Look around you. What things are frustrating you? Make a list of these things and what you could do to resolve them. There are HR leadership vacuums practically everywhere. If your list gets too long and becomes overwhelming:

-- Choose the highest priority item.

-- Force yourself to make the time.

-- Share your strategy with your boss.

-- Find someone to collaborate with.

-- Create a plan to get it done.

-- Then start taking itty-bitty, baby steps forward.

You'll be shocked at what you'll accomplish…and how great it will make you feel, not to mention those around you.

How to Turn Your Outrage & Frustration With Your Manager Into Your Next Promotion By
STEPPING UP!

Lori was an HR manager in our Quaker Oats Food Service Division and was an attendee at one of our annual HR National meetings. She was there with her boss and a number of her HR colleagues.

During a break in the meeting, she cornered me and asked: "Could I talk to you alone for a minute?" So she and I ducked out of the meeting room, went down the hall, and found an empty meeting room to step into.

"I am very, very frustrated," she told me.

"There are so many things we could be doing with our clients to move the business forward. We keep hearing about all these new HR best practices that all the other divisions are doing, but my boss never gets anything new implemented. Nothing happens. Our team knows that when he comes back from a big meeting like this and talks about all the new things other HR teams are doing, all we have to do is wait a few days and it'll all blow over."

"What kinds of things would you have him do?" I asked.

"Run some webinars for our managers on how to use our performance management system better, create an on-boarding program for our new hires, and do some retention risk assessments of our key talent to determine what we need to do to keep them. Also many of the other divisions have started looking into programs to address work life balance issues for working moms. We haven't done anything."

"Wait a minute," I said, raising my hand like a traffic cop and bringing her to a halt. "Lori, these all sound like excellent ideas to me and most don't require any senior management approval to implement. Right?"

"Right. But he won't do any of them," she said sadly.

"Well, Lori," I said, "*what are YOU waiting for?*"

For the first time that day, Lori was speechless. We didn't have time to continue our discussion so she returned to the meeting room with a dazed, but thoughtful look on her face.

You see, it's easy to complain about your manager's failure to take charge, pick up the ball and just run with it. And in this case, Lori was certainly justified in being frustrated by her boss's lack of initiative.

She told me she had complained to him and about him for over a year. And, she had been frustrated all that time.

Obviously, that wasn't going to change anything. So to me, her options were obvious.

One, accept him and the situation and stop being perturbed.

Two, continue to complain and feel frustrated every day as long as she reported to him.

Three, leave this job and this manager.

And four, step up, take charge and get some of these things going herself.

A lot of HR folks I've talked with would have chosen to accept the situation and take out their frustrations by either suffering in silence or continuing to complain.

A few would even try and sabotage their manager, which inevitably could backfire on them.

Not Lori.

About a year later, Lori and I connected again at another one of our division HR meetings. The night before, her manager -- the one that she had a problem with a year before -- privately raved about Lori to me over dinner and disclosed that he was planning to promote her.

The next day, Lori cornered me again on a break away from her manager. "I want to tell you," she began, "that I was very angry with you and the way you answered me that day. I wanted some sympathy. And frankly, I wanted you to go have a talk with my manager. But I sure didn't want you to challenge me."

"Should I apologize?" I asked.

"Not at all," she answered.

"Let me tell you about what's happened in the last year. I started running 'Performance Management & Leadership,' training sessions and have taken over 50 managers through this program. It covers writing objectives, coaching employees, and doing year-end performance reviews. Our managers are thrilled with the sessions. I worked with our OD people to develop a new on-boarding program for new hourly hires which has already begun to lower our turnover rate. I contacted one of our sister divisions and they agreed to not only share their work life program with us but they've helped us put on some lunch and learn sessions with our working moms on work life balance."

"I'm excited about what we've accomplished. I'm through waiting for things to happen. I'm now stepping up."

That's great for Lori. Now, what about YOU. What are you waiting for?

Embrace Unexpected HR Opportunities, Even If You Aren't 100% Ready For Them!

The number one thing I consistently see that slows down savvy HR folks is their own reluctance to accept a career opportunity simply because they don't think they're ready.

When does this happen?

Anytime.

It could happen if you're offered that "once-in-a-lifetime" big promotion to China that you've hoped for.

It could happen if you're asked to lead a major company-wide task force on improving employee engagement.

It could happen if one of your clients, a powerful senior executive, taps you on the shoulder and asks you for some specific, direct feedback on how she can work better with her team.

In cases like this, it's natural to doubt yourself and question whether you have what it takes.

But the truth is nobody ever feels 100% ready when a big opportunity arises.

Why?

Because most great opportunities jerk us out of our comfort zone and force us to stretch ourselves emotionally and intellectually, which means we won't feel totally comfortable at first. And when we don't feel comfortable, we darn sure don't feel ready.

Significant moments of opportunity will land at your doorstep throughout your career in HR.

However, to win BIG in your HR career you will need to take advantage of these sudden "moments" of opportunity...even though you will never feel COMPLETELY prepared and ready for them.

"Faith is taking the first step...even when you can't see the entire staircase! "
--Dr. Martin Luther King, Jr.

Here are the steps involved in STEPPING UP:

Big steps.
Little steps.
Step up.
Step down.
Side step.
In step.
Out of step.
Over step.
Step aside.
Giant step.
Back step.
Step away.
Baby steps.
Step out.
Step in it.
A step ahead.
Major steps.
First steps.
Next steps.
Step by step.
Step it up.
One step forward – two steps back.

Steps come in many forms, shapes and sizes.

What's your next step?

Give A Damn!

How To Get People To Give A Damn About You, Your Ideas & Your HR Career!

First Of All, Start Giving A Damn About THEM!

Stop talking about yourself, your problems and your own interests so damn much.

Being a self-centered jerk is not a recipe for success.

Start talking in ways that benefit other people and you'll start attracting attention and building credibility.

For example: If you're selling the idea of using social media in recruiting, it's not about how it will enable you to create a state-of-the-art talent acquisition system in your organization (which will look good at your year-end performance review). It's all about how it can allow your busy clients to find hard-to-hire candidates faster.

Another example: If you're trying to get a reluctant manager to attend an in-house leadership development seminar, it's not about how it will allow HR to achieve their objective of getting

100% attendance in the program. It's about how the program will address that manager's horrible and embarrassing 360 results. Or how it will build that manager's personal network of contacts within the organization which will enable them to be more productive. Or, even how it will benefit that manager, politically, by demonstrating to the "powers-that-be" about how serious they are about their own development.

That's what it's _really_ all about.

If you're telling your clients anything other than what your HR idea or program can do for THEM, then you're telling the *wrong story*.

Instead, set yourself up as the solution to your client's problems and you've made an important step in being perceived as a winner they want to associate with.

Start Solving Real Damn HR Problems With Real Damn Solutions!

Often, HR pros act as speed bumps to progress by failing to provide real fixes to organization issues.

For example, one of the biggest mistakes made is with employee onboarding.

In most organizations, HR runs the new employee orientation program…a program that most employees find boring and utterly forgettable.

Yet, we continue to do this when we know damn well that great on-boarding is a *process,* not a half-day *program* with donuts and highly caffeinated in-house speakers.

If we were to solve the real problem with onboarding, we would focus instead on providing the best resources and tools that help employees get up to speed on how to do their job as quickly as possible.

That's an example of a *real* solution.

The point: provide real answers to real issues. That's how you become irresistible and build trust and goodwill with your clients and others who can get you where you want to go.

Focus On Making Just One Tiny Little Damn Difference In People's Lives Everyday!

Several years ago I attended a lecture by Richard Carlson author of numerous books, the most famous of which was *Don't Sweat the Small Stuff.*

I don't remember much about his talk...except one thing. It happened to be the simplest suggestion he made, the one that required the smallest change.

That suggestion was to try every single day to make one tiny difference in someone else's life.

Each of us has numerous opportunities to affect lives of others or the world in general.

Each day when people cross our path -- the boss, colleagues, clients, friends and relatives -- they give us the opportunity to touch them in a positive way. And we can offer them:

- a kind word
- a special favor
- positive acknowledgment
- a simple smile
- a listening ear
- an open mind
- a receptive heart
- encouragement
- belief in them and their ideas, goals and dreams
- tough love

There is much more I could add this list, but I'm sure you get the point. We don't have to be CHRO's, multi-millionaire HR consultants or powerful influential HR leaders to positively impact others. Each of us in our own way has something very special we can offer other people.

You may never know how a kind word from you at just the right moment or a little encouragement during tough times can have on the rest of their day or life. There are so many ways you can touch people. You can share your gifts of energy, ideas, time, counsel, love, support and belief to help them along their journey.

However, there is one key to making this all work. When you do small things for people, do them...

With no intention of ever, ever, ever being repaid.

Why? Because givers, get. Just not on your time schedule. But eventually it happens. I can't explain it. I don't have all the scientific evidence. I know it just happens. Reciprocation works. Just not in the way you intended. Just recognize that when you do someone a favor, they are more likely to return it. In their mind, subconsciously you become more important to them and more worthy of their time.

Damn It, Stop Using Overhyped Buzz-Words To Describe Yourself!

Do you describe yourself as a *"result-oriented"* HR generalist with a *"dynamic proven track record?"* Or something similar.

My suggestion: Stop it! Please. Trash the buzz-words.

Here's why.

LinkedIn recently did an analysis of the profiles of its 85 million users and came up with a list of the most overused words and expressions. Here are their top ten:

1. Extensive experience
2. Innovative
3. Motivated
4. Results-oriented

5. Dynamic
6. Proven track record
7. Team player
8. Fast-paced
9. Problem solver
10. Entrepreneurial

The LinkedIn study validates what I've suspected for years, which is that certain overused HR words and phrases have no absolutely effect on executives, your clients or hiring managers. None at all. Using them just tells them that you're boring, forgettable and just like everyone else.

It lets them know that you don't stand for anything unique.

So do yourself a favor. Find new ways to describe your brilliance. For example, as an alternative, try asking yourself: "When someone reads my resume or company profile, can the reader say without hesitation why I should matter to them?"

If you can't define who you are and why you matter, then you and your career are dying a slow death…and you may not even know it. Take time to stop the bleeding.

Start Being Your Own Damn Self. Everyone Else Is Taken!

Some years ago, I was at lunch in Chicago in a fancy restaurant, with some Pepsi HR big wigs from our New York corporate office. When the salads came, there were too many forks on the table to choose from, and I wasn't quick enough to watch which one everyone else picked up. I was honestly confused. So I asked the guy next to me which fork to start with. About six months later, this guy transferred to Chicago and became my boss. He told me that, at that moment at lunch, even though he'd never met me before his trust in me skyrocketed, simply because I was unafraid to admit

I didn't know something – in that case which fork to use. (I've since learned the "from-the-outside-in" rule)

My lesson from that experience: Never underestimate the power of being yourself – and how truly attractive that can be to other people.

Lots of HR people walk on eggshells these days. They bury who they really are. They're not authentic. They're uncomfortable revealing parts of themselves they'd love to share with others. They do this because they believe their organizations don't really value their uniqueness. Or, they fear they'll get biased treatment. And in many cases, they're right.

However, to win big in HR, you must be able to bring your "whole" self to work. Here's why: unless you're in a Broadway play, it's too confusing and exhausting to play one role by day, be yourself at night and sustain your "A" game. And you need to tap into every ounce of energy you have if you're going to compete with the best and brightest in your organization every day.

At one time, many of us were trained to sanitize our resumes -- removing any trace of our ethnicity, sexual orientation or cultural heritage for fear that we wouldn't be interviewed. Today, that's still a very real risk in some organizations, though increasingly less so. But, if you're going to find a place where you can thrive and make an "emotional investment" in the company's success, you're going to need to take a risk – maybe even a big one. That means feeling comfortable talking about that pick-up basketball game you played in the inner city on weekends instead of golf. It means being comfortable sharing your activities in the Gay Pride events in your town.

I will make no pretense that any of this is easy to do or will be embraced with open arms by everyone. But it's necessary if you want to find an organization that you can embrace fully, feel passionate about and excel in.

Stop Being Afraid To Find Your Real Damn HR Mission In Life!

It's time to lose those beliefs that have put your career in a box. They've run your life for long enough. You're great enough, talented enough and, yes, you deserve to totally enjoy your HR career.

Here's how: Decide who you are and who you aren't. Write down precisely what distinguishes you from the rest of the HR folks who do something similar — in your company or elsewhere. Brand yourself and add these words to it: "....*and nobody does it better.*" Don't spend a whole lot of time beating yourself up over what did or didn't work in the past. Let it go so you can live and work in the present. Be in the here and now.

When I ended my PepsiCo HR career in 2008, and outed myself as an author, speaker and career advisor to HR professionals, I was clueless as to what would happen next. However, I followed my gut and did what came naturally. I started a blog. I wrote my first book. I began doing some consulting with Human Resources clients and took tiny steps towards following the dream I had buried for years.

And some remarkable things started happening in my life.

People started offering me full-time HR jobs.

People started offering me money to speak.

Companies offered me money to do HR consulting.

Since leaving the corporate jungle for good, and during the worst recession in 80 years, I've turned down more jobs and business opportunities than I ever imagined. I don't say all this to brag, but to illustrate the power of focusing on one's real mission. To be honest, I mostly walked away from these opportunities because I knew I'd be doing stuff I hated doing. Instead, I stuck to my plan and focused on my loves: writing, speaking and consulting.

As a result, I'm having a B-L-A-S-T!!!

Listen, I'm not saying that everyone can be like me. Being me definitely has its ups & downs. But you can grow and excel in your HR career — by simply being more like <u>YOU</u>, finding your own damn mission and following it.

Don't Allow People To Treat You Like A Damn Doormat!

Intentionally or not, consciously or not, you are constantly teaching people how to treat you (via your actions and reactions).

Being nice is one thing, but being a urinal for others is another.

Get some balls.

Some people are toxic.

They'll drain the life-force from your body and then dance on your rotting carcass…if you let them.

Some people are attention-seeking, high-maintenance energy vampires. Other than that, they're awesome! So choose your friends and close colleagues carefully.

Take Damn Good Care Of Yourself!

Have more fun. HR folks who never have fun are boring and miserable. And, people run the other way from the boring and the miserable. Apart from the numerous mental, emotional and social benefits of fun, it also leads to a stronger immune system, less sickness and faster recovery time when we do get ill.

Don't feed your mind crap. Like your body, your mind also has a voracious appetite. It is constantly consuming and digesting information. If you fill your mind with negative stuff, it will become a negative place to live. And, yes, your mind is mostly where you "live." Your body is merely a form of transport for your mind and spirit. And, carrying negative stuff around with you constantly just drives others in the opposite direction.

Stop doing destructive crap to your body. You can get a new job, house, car and spouse but you can't get a new body. So get off the couch, fatso. Move your arms and legs. Do bad stuff to your body and it will do worse stuff to you and your attractiveness to others.

Damn It, Don't Make It About Black, Brown, White Or Any Other Color Except Green!

Regarding your race, accept the fact that life isn't fair. Fair is something that you pay when you jump in a taxi (i.e. fare).

You make your own breaks.

Don't worry about why you were hired. You could be hired in HR because the diversity plan calls for bringing in a Black female. The guy next to you could be hired because he's the CEO's White godson. You were both hired because of your ethnicities. But so what? You both got in. Congratulations!

Now that you're in, focus on distinguishing yourself by figuring out ways to help your business generate more of the green stuff. As an HR pro, make building your financial acumen and delivering value priority one.

Will that eliminate bias and make things fair? Probably not. You may still feel your mistakes are magnified more than those of others. You may still be misperceived, misinterpreted or even stereotyped on occasion. You may still have to be better adept at building alliances and marketing your accomplishments in order to succeed.

However, you can waste precious time grousing about the unfairness of it all, or you can invest that same time making yourself indispensable. Of course, today no one really is irreplaceable. But by directing your HR attention on ways to help your organization deliver their business plan, reduce costs, and improve their competitiveness, you can become a valuable, tough-to-replace commodity…the type of commodity companies want to keep…no matter what you look like.

There you have it, a few doses of politically incorrect advice to make your clients, colleagues and others captivated by you, smitten with your ideas and anxious to help carry the torch for your HR career.

Of course, some of you will be offended and bothered by my language, my biases and my message. But, fortunately for me…

…I don't give a damn. 🙂

You're welcome.

Own Your HR Career!

You Are In Business For Yourself!

No matter how you make your living in HR or which organization you work for, you really only work for one person.

YOURSELF.

The big question is: What are you selling and to whom? Even if you have a full-time, salaried position in a Fortune 500 company, you are still running your own business. The only difference is that YOU are the "product" and you're selling the following:

- One unit of your existence (*an hour of your life*)
- At a set price (*the associated fraction of your salary*)
- To a big customer (*your employer*)
- Populated with consumers who must be blown away by the value you provide (*your clients*).

So how can you become a more valuable product? It's simple.

Solve more problems. Produce more solutions.

Clients and organizations love HR people who are proactive, flexible problem-solvers.

What kind of problems should you solve? That's easy. You should be tackling the biggest issues that plague your organization or your clients the most.

If you have the choice of pushing back, grousing and complaining about why these problems exist in the first place…or jumping in the mix, positioning yourself as a "solution provider" and building your HR brand in the process. I say opt for the latter.

But let's get real. Chances are no matter how much value you're adding, if the business goes belly up, you can expect to get canned. But just because you lose your job doesn't mean that you lose all your experiences, talents, ideas, leadership and determination. Again, you are a business.

You are not your job, so don't lose your identity in it.

Your job isn't your security blanket.

Your one-person business is.

The Single Most Important Step In Winning Big & Attaining True Greatness In HR!

Years ago, I was advised to get a law degree to advance my career in HR.

So, I studied for the LSAT exam. Took the test. Got a decent score. Then I applied to the John Marshall law school in Chicago.

And got accepted.

My plan was to work my HR job by day. And take my law school classes by night. And then juggle all the demands of being a full-time HR generalist and my young family in-between.

All this would take me four years.

I had a well thought out game plan.

Simple. Right?

Well…a funny thing happened just before I was to start my first semester of classes.

I started REALLY thinking about what I had just gotten myself into. It consumed my thoughts during the day.

And, gave me a lot of sleepless nights.

My intuition — and that knot in my stomach — was trying to tell me something.

By then, I had learned to listen to my gut.

And it was screaming at me loudly and clearly.

So, I made a BIG decision…

I quit law school.

I quit before I even got started.

I quit two days before I ever attended a single class.

Why, you say?

Well, it wasn't because I didn't want to put in the work.

The reason was even more basic…

I was an HR guy. And deep down, I had absolutely <u>NO</u> freaking desire to be a lawyer.

Nada. Zero. Zip.

In fact, the entire field of law had no appeal to me whatsoever.

Though I respected lawyers, I really didn't want to be one.

Sure, I knew that many of the most senior HR executives at my company at the time had law degrees. In fact, when I asked for career advice, many of them told me: "Go to law school. It'll really help you at this company. Besides, you'll make a great attorney."

Flattered, I had decided to follow their advice.

They told me that it didn't matter that I already had a master's degree in Industrial Relations from Purdue. I needed to punch the ticket and have that law degree too...especially if I wanted "an edge" in my HR career.

I realize now, many years later, that had I gone ahead with my law school plans that I would have been miserable. Totally.

I would have let others steer me away from my true passions and career aspirations in HR. Those that I strongly believed in, both then and now.

In retrospect, this all looks really stupid now. Especially, when I consider that all of these people whose opinions I cared so much about at the time are no longer a part of my life. And that steel company that I worked so hard in for eight long years, no longer even exists.

Ultimately, I joined Quaker Oats then PepsiCo and discovered after a few years there, my educational credentials were the LEAST important contributor to my ultimate success in HR.

From this episode, I learned an important career lesson.

Unfortunately, just before you take your first step on the righteous journey to pursue your dreams in HR, many people around you, even the ones who deeply care for you, will usually give you absolutely <u>awful</u> career advice.

It's not because they have evil intentions.

It's not because they're idiots.

It's because they often don't take the time to understand what YOU really want to achieve – and what YOUR dreams, passions and life goals mean to you.

Sometimes, even you don't know what you want – beyond just saying: "I want to be successful. I want to move up. I want to make more money."

And, frankly, it is that lack of clarity that is a big part of the problem.

Because in reality, there is no <u>ONE</u> proven path to greatness in HR…EXCEPT to find a way to spend your time doing what creates enjoyment for you and others.

If you don't want to, you DON'T have to become a CHRO or make millions in base salary in a Fortune 50 company to achieve greatness in HR.

If you don't want to, you DON'T have to work 100-hour weeks for years doing stuff you hate to achieve true greatness in HR.

It's ok to say NO to someone else's career ladder and still wind up on top.

You merely have to <u>CLEARLY</u> figure out what greatness means for YOU. And then work towards it.

That's it.

You have to be able to close your eyes and picture what kind of career in HR would make you the most happy and fulfilled. What would you be doing? Who would you be working with? How would you be spending your day? You must be able to define it and then start taking steps every day to work towards that vision.

That's first step towards attaining <u>true</u> greatness in HR.

Define your personal vision of success and chart YOUR own path. Then man-up and own it!

Stop caring about what everyone else wants for you.

Stop concerning yourself with what everyone else's opinion is about your career.

Don't get me wrong. It's great to have mentors, advisors, supporters and fans. It's important to listen to their advice and consider it carefully. But then...

Decide On What <u>YOU</u> Want And Then Pursue It Aggressively!

Keep in mind what the great Steve Jobs said, five years before his death:

"Your time on earth is limited, so don't waste it living someone else's life. Don't be trapped by dogma, which is living with the results of other people's thinking. Don't let the noise of others' opinions drown out your own inner voice, heart and intuition – because somehow it already knows what you truly want to become. Everything else is secondary."

Go ahead. Read Steve's quote one more time.

It's that brilliant.

And the best career advice you'll ever receive.

Decide that you will become the BEST POSSIBLE YOU.

You can't be anyone else.

That's the single most important path to winning big in HR.

And it's waiting for you.

Reframe Failure!

Failing In HR Is A Detour, <u>Not</u> A Dead End Street.

Winners in Human Resources accept their failures, disappointments and setbacks and continue on. They know that failure is only a natural consequence of trying – NOT a final defeat.

Winning in HR Always Involves Some Failures Along The Way.

From my talks with many top HR executives, I've learned (usually after a round of adult beverages) that they all share one common theme: If they're had off-the-charts success in HR, they've failed too. Lots of times. You and I just may not know about them. The world rewards successes and so many of them just choose not to walk around bragging and publicizing their screw-ups. Just for kicks, let me share some of my own failures and setbacks from my 25 years in HR:

- **I've interviewed for 24 different HR jobs I did NOT get.**
- I've been passed over 7 times for HR promotions that I thought I was an absolute lock for.
- **I've gotten performance ratings more horrible than I expected on 6 occasions.**
- I've hired 6 "high potential" HR people for my team that I later had to fire for poor performance.
- **I've had 4 big shot senior executives who hated my guts bad mouth me to my boss.**
- I've led 3 management-union labor negotiations that resulted in embarrassing, nasty strikes that I didn't anticipate.
- I've facilitated lots of off-site client meetings (too many to mention) that ended up in the toilet.
- **I've had so many of my best HR ideas rejected by upper management that I've lost count.**

Here is what's remarkable about this list: Just about every one of these disappointments later set the stage for my BIGGEST HR career breakthroughs and successes.

So, if you've failed in anything lately in HR, my hat's off to you. Congratulations! You're probably well on your way towards your next success.

TWO Lessons The World's Biggest Failures Can Teach You About Winning Big In HR

Here's a short list of world famous flops:

- **Steve Jobs** was fired from Apple – a company he co-founded.
- **J.K. Rowling**, author of the *Harry Potter* series has sold 400 million books, but only after she was rejected by 12 publishers.
- **Michael Jordan** as a high school sophomore failed to make his varsity basketball team — another sophomore beat him out.
- **Walt Disney** was fired from a newspaper because "he had no new ideas and lacked imagination."
- **Winston Churchill** failed 6th grade and lost every election for public office, until he won and became the Prime Minister of the United Kingdom during the Second World War.
- **Jennifer Hudson** was beaten by 6 other singers on *American Idol*. Three years later as a singer in the movie *Dream Girls,* she won an Academy Award for her performance.
- **Barack Obama** was soundly defeated in his first race for U.S. Congress and began as an underdog behind Hillary Clinton and John Edwards in his run for White House -- before getting elected as the first black President of the United States.

The TWO lessons for you as an HR pro:

1. **Like people in any other profession, in HR, no matter how great you are, you <u>WILL</u> experience failure.**
2. **When that happens, no matter how painful it is...DON'T GIVE UP!** You may need a different approach, more training, a mentor, a partner, or wait for a different time, but continue to **PERSIST** and **TAKE ACTION** in the direction of your dreams and ambitions.

A Powerful Story of Attaining Great Career Success in HR -- Despite Brutal and "Impossible" Odds!

Steve Pemberton (*pictured below*) is an awesome HR leader.

At the time this book is being written, he's recognized as one of the nation's leaders in diversity and inclusion.

He is Chief Diversity Officer and Divisional VP for Walgreens.

In 2006, *Fortune* magazine named him as one of the Top 20 Chief Diversity Officers in America.

In 2007, Steve was called to Capitol Hill to provide expert testimony on best practices in diversity recruiting.

And in 2008, he was named by *Savoy* as one of The Top 100 most influential African-Americans in corporate America.

Steve currently serves on several boards including The Home for Little Wanderers and UCAN to provide guidance and inspiration to children in need.

The *Pemberton Fund for the Future* has been established at The Home for Little Wanderers to assist children aging out of the foster care system.

CLEARLY, STEVE HAS ATTAINED SUPER-STARDOM IN OUR PROFESSION.

...BUT THAT'S <u>NOT</u> THE MOST REMARKABLE PART OF HIS STORY!

THIS IS...

- **He was abandoned by his mother at age three and lived an utterly terrifying existence as a child.**
- He was bounced from one foster family to another. Finally he was adopted by a cruel foster family that subjected him to constant abuse.
- **That family, the Robinsons, can only be described as monsters.**
- They subjected him to merciless beatings.
- **They made deliberate attempts to block him from progressing academically.**
- While living with them, he was hungry — seemingly always hungry — but was not permitted to open the refrigerator – ever!
- **He was required to adhere to a series of *Robinson Family Rules* which included: #1-You are to never tell anyone outside this house about what goes on here. #2-We aren't your mother and father. You call us ma'am and sir. #4-You are dumb, and ugly. Something about you isn't right. Everybody knows this. #7-We can beat you at any moment. #8-No one wants you, especially your own mother and father.**
- As a child, to survive, he was only able to find refuge in books. And a kind neighbor, who saw a spark in him, noticed his interest in reading, and gave him more books to read. But what the neighbor didn't know was that Steve was only permitted to read in a cold, dark, dank basement.

However, it was in reading and learning from these books, that he discovered new worlds and perspectives...and gained the hope that one day he might have a different life and find his true home and calling.

Armed with just a single clue, Steve embarked on an extraordinary quest to find his real identity…but found that nothing was quite as it appeared.

Steve has captured this and other aspects of his amazing story in his brilliant book called: *A Chance In The World: An Orphan Boy, a Mysterious Past, and How He Found a Place Called Home.* It is a riveting autobiography that chronicles his horrific childhood, his difficult path through foster care and his determined search for his family. It is an inspirational story that crosses generations and cultures and speaks to those who have had the odds stacked against them. Steve's relentless journey to overcome his childhood, find his biological family and right the wrongs of his parents' past, is a model for all families to follow. It is a true testament to his faith, fortitude and forgiveness.

I'm going to go out on a limb and say that the obstacles you currently face in attaining your career goals in Human Resources are NOTHING compared to what Steve has faced in reaching his.

If that's true, then you have two choices:

1. **You can let your own handicaps roadblock you, imprison your HR career ambitions or force you to give up…OR…**

2. **You can learn from your HR disadvantages, barriers and shortcomings. You can regard them as merely temporary setbacks and continue to *persist* and *take action*. And recognize that the breakthrough you're looking for in your HR career is just around the corner.**

The faster you accept this, the faster you can get on with being brilliant and winning big as Steve Pemberton now has.

The choice is yours.

Know Your Business Cold!

Make Sure You Can Pass The Blackboard Test!

Decades ago, when Lee Iacocca took over Chrysler, he spent the first week calling people into his office and gave them the "blackboard test."

He told them to go over to a chalkboard and take 7 minutes to diagram how whatever they did directly contributed to Chrysler's primary business...which was selling cars. Anybody that couldn't draw a clear diagram was fired.

As an HR professional, if you know your business cold, you should have no problem passing your own CEO's blackboard test. Can you? That should be your goal.

"It's Easy To Impress Your Clients With Your Knowledge Of HR, When You've Impressed Them With Your Knowledge Of THEIR Business First!"

Anyone that wins BIG in HR does so by first getting brilliant on their business. I don't mean the HR business. But the business that is providing you with a paycheck. Succeeding in HR requires high degrees of influence with business leaders. And that only comes by knowing your business well enough that you can tie your HR initiatives to the business and leverage them to move that business forward.

Wanted Desperately: Strong, Decisive, Courageous, Kick-Butt HR Leaders! Wimps Need NOT Apply.

John Doyle, who leads HR executive search for Spencer Stuart put it best: "If I ask a potential HR candidate, 'So how are things with you?' and they tell me that they have just launched a new employee engagement program, I know I'm not talking to the right person. But if they tell me, without hesitation, about the business -- growth opportunities, revenues and earnings, for example -- I know I'm on the right track." According to Doyle: **"Pleasant, polite, consensus-building HR pros are fine. But they're a dime a dozen. However, kick-butt, decisive HR leaders, who know the business cold, can get people to follow them, and make things happen are GOLDEN."**

Drop the HR Jargon!

It is a mistake to think that speaking HR psychobabble, or giving "HR opinions" and "HR perceptions," without conveying how your idea touches the P&L, will carry much weight when trying to gain credibility with your business leaders. Many HR professionals aren't numbers people. But you should be. Speaking in numbers, not words, elevates your status. **Numbers and dollars are the language of business.** And to earn your seat at the table with your leadership team, you should NOT treat this as a foreign language.

Speak Up On Business Issues!

Be a business person first, an HR person second. Have points of view about the business and don't hesitate to share them. Don't behave like your clients have all of the answers. When leadership meetings shift from talking talent to talking business, many HR folks take that as their cue to shut up, check their e-mail messages under the table or leave the room entirely. Why? Because they really don't know the business, they lack confidence or they're afraid of their clients pushing back. This is a great way of being shoved to the side by the big boys and girls when the "real" decisions need to be made…and having your business to lose out on the full HR perspective. Isn't speaking up and contributing to business discussions risky? Sure it is. But your business leaders will respect you and seek out your counsel, especially if you've:

- Done your homework
- Listen well
- Make your comments fact-based and meaningful
- Tie them to the REAL needs of the organization.

Make Sure You Can Survive The Elevator Ride!

"The elevator ride" has become a legendary tale in the Silicon Valley. Now, I don't know if this story is true or not. But people still talk about it to this day.

Here's how Ed Niehaus, a senior executive at Apple who witnessed the incident, describes it:

"An employee got on the elevator with Steve Jobs, then CEO at Apple. I could see her go, 'oops, wrong elevator.' And Steve said, 'Hi, who are you?' and introduces himself to her - 'I'm Steve Jobs'. Then turning on the charm he said, 'What do you do?' She explains. After 15 seconds, the door of the elevator opens, and he says, 'We are not going to need you. You're fired.' And he walks away."

End of story. End of the elevator ride. End of her career at Apple

Here's the question that's important to YOU:

1. As an HR professional, could you survive the "Steve Jobs' elevator ride" if it were your CEO in the elevator?

2. From your CEO's perspective, is what you do in HR essential to the business?

3. If so, what would you say on that elevator ride?

If you can't answer these questions well, you're not adding enough value or making the kind of impact you should.

And, you've got work to do. Just sayin'.

(*A caveat:* As an HR guy, I'm personally not a big fan of what Jobs or Iacocca (see #21) did in these situations. Though each of them were truly business geniuses, giving the old "surprise goodbye" without prior notice, candid feedback and a rigorously candid performance evaluations is not my cup of tea. It's also not good for the company culture and it'll give your Legal Department fits. However, that's not the point here. The point is that each of these are tests of your ability to KNOW YOUR BUSINESS COLD. So what say you? Do you?)

15 Things Every Winner in HR Knows About Their Business!

1. They know how their company makes money.
2. They understand the difference between the firm's profit and cash.
3. They understand why the balance sheet balances.
4. The numbers neither scare nor mystify them.
5. They can talk about the company's share price (if it is publicly traded) and its most recent up and down trends.
6. They can state company's profit (bottom line) over the last two years.
7. They know the revenue growth (top line) over the last two years.
8. They understand the business' key productivity (cost management) metrics and strategies.
9. They can answer questions about the primary product brands or services offered.
10. They can tell you how their top customers are being satisfied.
11. They can describe how the product is manufactured or the service is delivered.
12. They've learned how products/services are developed, marketed and sold.
13. They know their key suppliers and customers.
14. They can describe the key retention and attraction strategies for the top customers.
15. They know what gives their company a competitive advantage.

An Example Of "Going The Extra Mile" By Using The Financials To Justify An HR Program!

Let's say you want to add a new kiosk at one of your manufacturing plants, so that your employees can have direct access to their payroll, benefits and compensation information.

Your boss says he'll listen, but he wants you to justify the purchase.

Money's tight.

You can certainly provide "soft" data from your most recent employee survey.

And, there's nothing wrong with that.

That's what most HR folks would do.

However, the HR winner will go "one step farther" and also dig up data from finance, including the costs, cash flow analysis for the kiosk, working capital requirements, ROI, and a depreciation schedule.

Most of these numbers -- surprise! -- are based on assumptions and estimates.

The HR pro will then make sure these numbers make sense with the help of their finance counterpart (who they've partnered with). If not, then the assumptions and estimates are adjusted so that they're more realistic and support the proposal.

There are a variety of assumptions that can be made. In this case let's say they assume that they can save an hour a day per employee because of the new computer's features and processing speed. And, based on this, they calculate the value of an hour per day of his time over a year. Presto! The recommendation shows that buying the kiosk is a no-brainer.

It's then presented, approved and implemented.

The result helps the business and the employees.

And the use of the financials helped make it all happen!

The #1 Acid Test For Demonstrating Your Knowledge Of The Business!

Could you fill in for your business leader for 30 minutes if you were asked to?

Let's say, you're an HR director in the Gatorade business at Pepsi, and your Gatorade general manager was out sick, could you step in and give his 30 minute monthly financial update to the leadership team?

Could you describe the current challenges facing the business?

Or talk with confidence about how Gatorade is made, where it's made, how it makes money, and how the product has been positioned to attract consumers in the marketplace?

And could you describe the P&L impact of the HR programs and initiatives you're accountable for.

Tough standard? Yes.

Impossible? Definitely not.

At PepsiCo, we called this "knowing the business cold" and all of our very best HR people – the ones that were true partners with their business leaders — had this skill in spades.

And you'd be amazed that how much credibility they had, how much they were valued and how much they were (and are) able to influence the performance their business. This should be your goal.

Seven Ways To Build Your Business Know-How...FAST!

Get Out in the Trenches!

(1) If your company has manufacturing plants, get out on the floor with the folks on the frontline who make the product. Talk to them about THEIR issues, not yours. As a junior HR general-generalist, I was told: *"You need to get out and walk the plant floor on regular basis. That's the best way of getting a pulse beat on the business. In fact, if you don't have to get a new pair of safety shoes every six months, you're not doing your job."*

(2) Get some of your sales reps to let you go on sales calls with them to learn the needs of the customers and consumers of your business. Or set aside a few hours on a regular basis and watch how your customer service reps work with irate customer calls. Customers are the lifeblood of any organization.

(3) Whenever possible, set up routine meetings with your colleagues in Purchasing, Engineering, Marketing and R&D on their turf (not yours) to learn the challenges they face in their area of the organization. Make this one of your weekly priorities.

Start a Reading Program!

Become familiar with the strategic business plans for your unit.

Read your company's annual report. Read the same industry trade publications or investor reports that your business leaders read.

Beef up your grasp of balance sheets and P&L statements. To help, you may want to google: *"How To Read A Financial Report"* published by Merrill Lynch and download it online.

Make Friends with Finance!

You don't have to bug the crap out of your CFO. Instead, find a financial manager who helps pull the numbers that show how the business is performing. Lunch and learn with him or her. Get their coaching on how your business makes money. Build a relationship. Offer to return the favor by becoming a resource to them on HR issues.

Bond with Investor Relations!

If you're in a publicly traded company, the folks in the Investor Relations (IR) group are the key story tellers who have to explain to shareholders everything from the latest SEC filing to the quarterly earnings or latest product launches. When they're not scrambling to meet a disclosure deadline, schedule a working lunch with them to understand the big picture. Pay for their meal. It's time and money well spent.

Get on the Distribution Lists!

Many Finance, IR, Strategy or Competitive Intelligence functions in companies have distribution lists for financial updates, analyst reports, competitor news and legislative and regulatory issues.

Get on the list (often it's the same list for everyone). If the data is good enough for your business leaders, it's good enough for you. If you find it tough to get copied on the distribution list, ask your business leader or your CHRO to make the request for you.

Wire Yourself!

Gather your own news and insights. Subscribe to RSS feeds or Google alerts on what's being written in social media about your company, its competitors and your industry. This puts you in the know as fast as any senior executive in your company. Knowledge is power. Don't rely only on what others can gather for you.

Tune in to Earnings Calls!

If you're in a publically traded company, listen to the quarterly earnings call with the analysts...especially the Q&A segment at the end of the call. Or read the transcripts. It's a good way to get a concise recap of the strategy story that your company is telling and gain insights on what investors – and your business leaders — are excited and worried about.

If you DON'T know your business cold, you will forever be relegated to the back of the bus in your organization.
And that's not where you need to be.

Your business desperately needs you as an HR pro upfront with your hands on the wheel helping to steer the bus.

It's the only way <u>THEY</u> can win
and <u>YOU</u> can win...BIG!

Become
Your Client's
Trusted Advisor!

10 Ways To Get Your Clients To Rave About You As An HR Pro...

Every client is different. Treat them accordingly. Winners in HR know that **the key to getting 'client love' is to know deep down what your clients REALLY want, WHEN they want it and then supply it to them.**

1. Sometimes your clients just want you to provide them with a step-by-step process to follow on their own. Provide it and step away.

2. **Sometimes your clients want an ear. If so, just listen, hear them out, be their sounding board and they will feel well served.**

3. Sometimes your clients just want you to check in with them, ask how they are and offer them some extra time and help.

4. Sometimes your clients need your support and validation that what they are doing is right or that they're on the right track.

5. Sometimes your clients don't want you to bother them at all. They want independence, so give them their space.

6. **Sometimes your clients want to know that you're available 24/7 if they need to call you. Most of them will never call, but knowing they can is good enough.**

7. Sometimes your clients want you to connect them to the right people: HR specialists, consultants, coaches, your colleagues or your boss. Provide them access to your network.

8. Sometimes your clients want you to challenge them, ask more of them, instead of just being "supportive." Raise their bar, help them play a bigger game and they'll love you.

9. Sometimes clients like to be surprised with gifts. Almost everyone likes to get a surprise, just don't make it a bribe.

10. **FINALLY...sometimes your clients won't follow your HR advice, no matter how terrific it is. Don't take this personally. Accept this reality and focus on EVERYONE ELSE.**

Saying YES!
The Sneaky Little Secret For Running An HR Department Your Clients Will Love!

Here's a complaint I once got from a Plant Manager about one my of best HR managers who was assigned to his manufacturing site in St. Louis...

"I like her work. She's extremely bright. But she is just too damn hard to deal with. Everything is a freakin' fight. Anytime my managers ask her to do something, she challenges them. When she does act, she wants to do surveys and study everything to death or take the plant through this org behavior crap I studied in grad school. What she comes up with is great and generally works more times than not, but it takes much, much too long. Frankly, I'd settle for someone a little less talented but with a greater sense of urgency."

He then pinpointed the REAL issue: *"She is a perfectionist. If my solution to an HR issue is only 80-90% correct, she pushes back. I think she uses this as a substitute for taking action. Meanwhile, my problems go unresolved."*

When I shared this feedback with her, she wasn't surprised, but didn't know what to do. I suggested that she follow two simple client success secrets that wound up working well with this particular client. They were...

Secret Number One:
Give the client what they <u>WANT</u> first.
Secret Number Two:
Then, give them what they <u>NEED.</u>

Here are two examples to illustrate:

Example One: Let's say your client is concerned about keeping his 10 best people and wants to throw retention bonus money at them. You and I both know that, in most cases, this is just a band-aid that doesn't heal the real problem. And, you can push back, say no, and even fight the client on it. Or you could say YES, and make this solution EVEN BETTER. How? By getting him to agree that as part of the total solution, both of you will develop an overall retention plan which might include:

(1) Providing more recognition, visibility, atta-boys to these top performers for their accomplishments,

(2) Coaching them more and providing them with greater freedom and autonomy in making decisions, and

(3) Offering them more flexible work schedules, more time off or better work life balance, when and where you can.

In doing this, you've just now made the retention bonus part of a "more comprehensive solution" for enriching their job experience, making it more fulfilling and more likely that they won't leave the organization.

Example Two: Let's say your client is hell bent on sending Sarah, one of his direct reports, to a training program to improve her leadership skills. You can argue all day long that external training alone is not going to significantly enhance her leadership capability (and you're right). Or you can say YES, but make the solution EVEN BETTER by working with the client to:

(1) Find the best training program possible and,

(2) Put in place a follow up plan that would include mentoring, 360 feedback, and more frequent coaching by the him and individual accountability by Sarah to demonstrate improvement.

With these add-ons, you've now made the leadership program a piece of a "much larger plan" that stands a much better chance of improving her leadership success, rather than just implementing the client's solution alone.

In these two examples, the client's solutions weren't wrong. They were merely *incomplete*.

97% of client-proposed solutions in HR are like this.

So, don't kill your clients' ideas. It just pisses them off. Instead, BUILD ON THEM to create a more robust fix.

When you enhance their original solution, most clients will readily embrace the combined proposal and act.

One other thing: Accepting the client's solution doesn't make you a wimp. You are, though, if your client is recommending something immoral, illegal or violates the company's ethics or code of conduct. In that case, you shouldn't be so agreeable. Your job then is to push back hard, become their worst nightmare and get your boss involved if needed.

-#####-

Got Clients From Hell?
Here's How To Deal With Them!

Years ago, as a HR generalist, I had the delightful privilege of working with the client from hell.

Not a client from hell. THE client from hell.

This client was an SVP and the top dog in Operations for my division.

And I didn't know if this client hated HR people in general, or simple hated me in particular, but it seemed as if I couldn't do anything right.

I dreaded getting telephone calls from this guy. When his name would pop up on my caller ID, I sometimes felt like throwing up before picking up the phone.

Meetings were even worse. I'd lie awake the night before trying to figure out a way to avoid them.

I remember one tough discussion we had about getting candidates for a hard-to-fill engineering job. He was absolutely unforgiving:

"Are you guys going to fill this job anytime before I die of old age? I want to see some candidates tomorrow, NOT two weeks from now. Got it? Now, get out of my office!"

The easy way out would have been to say, "Yes sir. Got it. We'll do our best" and run out of there like a scared rabbit.

But I knew, without a miracle, there was absolutely no way he was going to have candidates the next day.

And if I failed to deliver, he'd be coming after me again the following day, pitchfork in hand.

I also knew that if I said no, he'd want to inflict more rage right there.

And he'd wind up picking up the phone to call my boss to scream at her.

So, I immediately said, "Let me make a quick call and see what I can do." He looked at me with disgust and said: "Sure, you guys in HR are all alike. Can't make a freaking decision."

Except freaking was not the word he used.

Ignoring his put down, I stepped out of his office, and called our overworked staffing department.

After doing some big time begging and pleading, they agreed to produce some candidates within three days.

I went back to the client and said, "I know you want to see some folks tomorrow, but we can get you candidates in here in three days?"

His answer: "Two days." To which I replied, "John, I can push our staffing group to two days. But there's no guarantee that you'll see anything but a warm body that won't meet the high standards we've set for this job. It'll waste your time and mine and we'll be back to square one. Give us three days and we'll nail it."

"Okay, but they'd better be awesome, or you're dog meat," was his reply.

When I reconnected with our staffing group, they weren't happy campers but they knew that I was dealing with a madman, and they understood. And they jumped through hoops and delivered some fantastic engineering candidates in three days. (*I also returned the favor by generously providing the donuts and coffee for the next two mornings on my dime, while letting their boss know how responsive they were under pressure*).

Looking back on this, I admit I didn't have an entirely happy client. And, I didn't have an entirely pleasant group of colleagues in the staffing department, either. But I had managed to explore some options and negotiate a solution without the client feeling a need to go over my head to my boss, and without my colleagues thinking I'd sold them down the river either.

And I lived to work another day…which, given the circumstances, was just fine by me.

If you find yourself in a similar situation, here are a few tips you'll want to keep in mind for managing your clients successfully — especially those from hell...

Even If Client is Unreasonable And Wants A Miracle, Avoid Firing Off A Fast NO!

Remember what I said earlier about running a YES department.

Some HR departments have built huge reputations for saying "NO" and being speed bumps to progress.

Some build their power base by playing cop, policy geek and compliance officer.

Don't fall in this trap!

Your main job is to build bridges and help move the business forward. And usually, saying NO stops the business dead in its tracks.

Instead of giving a flat no, negotiate your way to a YES. For example, if faced with a client's request for an unreasonable pay increase for one of their employees, say: "Here's what we can do. We can give Jill a within guidelines pay increase now, and then review her performance again in 6 months and make another pay adjustment then, if it's warranted. Will that meet your need?" Providing clients with options and choices works better than firing off quick NO's.

At Times, You Won't Click Even With Your Best Clients. So Don't Take It Personally. Life's Too Short!

I won't blow smoke at you. If you're like most HR people, every now and then, even your best clients will be demanding and sometimes won't hesitate to kick you in the butt.

Some of what will happen to you will not be fair.

Some of it will be frustrating.

The injustice of it all will sting.

But using these few occasions to rage against the machine and your transgressors only labels you as someone with a thin skin and not ready for prime time in HR.

In these situations, your best strategy is to just take your bad medicine, swallow it and keep putting one foot in front of the other…focusing on making tomorrow a better day.

Again, even with terrific clients, every day is not sunshine…no matter what organization you work in.

It's part of our profession.

Accept it and use these difficult situations in HR to grow.

Continue to give your clients the best advice you can.

Be there for them.

Over-deliver.

And, keep moving forward.

If Your Client Is Truly From Hell, Start Your Exit Strategy!

There's a difference between **demanding clients** and **clients from hell.**

95% of your clients are fine, perhaps challenging, but they don't have horns or carry a pitchfork. However, when you encounter that other 5% from down below, you'll will want to pull the plug on this assignment ASAP.

If you don't address a toxic client relationship head on, you won't succeed. So put an end to it!

As a paid HR professional, you have more important things to do than to be a daily punching bag for your clients.

Your options:

Transfer.

Post for a new job.

Discuss with your boss taking on another client group or a different assignment.

Leave the organization.

Or offer to job swap with some other unsuspecting HR colleague (hey, just kidding!).

Either way, whatever you do, don't fall in the trap of trying to fix this person.

Research conducted by the Center for Creative Leadership reveals that trying to change your client is an utter waste of time – especially if their behavior has been tolerated (or even rewarded) by the organization. So stop wishing he or she will change and put your own needs first.

If your exit from this role is going to take some time, don't be vindictive. Be patient and bide your time. Continue to give this jerk the same responsive, professional, value-added HR support that you always have. Just because you're getting crapped on, is no excuse to return the favor.

However, don't plan to stay in this role long. If times get tough in your organization and HR downsizing occurs, you never can tell how much weight this madman's perceptions will be given in HR layoff decisions.

Let me be clear: the "personal development," the "character building" and the "+5% ~~compensation bribe~~...er, salary increase" you might get to work with bad clients is overrated. It may sound great at the time, but isn't worth it. Whatever you gain developmentally is offset by the hit you take to your HR reputation, your personal self-esteem and your mental sanity.

So avoid toxic clients at all costs.

If you're in an impossible relationship with a client and you suspect that you're continually being disrespected and abused, deal with it immediately.

You deserve better.

Play Politics!

7 Tips For Getting Ahead Without Being That Sleazy, Back-Stabbing Little Jerk That Everyone Hates!

Many HR folks feel screwed when their hard work and long hours don't pay-off in career advancement.

However, at a certain point, working harder at your HR day gig is NOT going to move your career forward.

And, it's certainly not going to deliver the life and the professional satisfaction you want.

If you want to win BIG in just about any HR role, you do <u>NOT</u> have the luxury of opting out of corporate politics.

In fact, the larger the organization, the more you will need to acquire a skill that doesn't appear on any HR competency model. That skill is called…**political savvy.**

I know what you're thinking:

"Playing politics is sleazy."

"Business should be a meritocracy."

"I've never been good at office politics."

"I absolutely refuse to play the political game at work."

"My hard work and results should be enough to get me praised, raised and recognized."

To these folks I say…GROW UP!

Being politically savvy is all about knowing the key influencers, building alliances and helping people win! That's all it is.

Most HR folks are great at these things. And the superstars in HR are absolute masters of the game.

So give yourself permission to play politics.

Here are a few ways to succeed at the game:

Make Your Boss Your Biggest Ally!

This is where it all starts.

Be proactive with your boss.

Get to her before she comes to you.

Know her priorities cold.

Anticipate what she needs to know and provide it to her regularly.

Get smarter on the things that drive her success.

Follow up on your 360 results or take steps to correct any adverse client feedback you get, so your boss can be your advocate.

You don't want her to have to fight uphill political battles on your behalf.

Or have to debate the perceptions that you're a jerk.

The last thing you'll want is to make it difficult for your boss to champion you when an opportunity arises.

Know The Key Influencers And Become Their Ally!

In every organization, there are influencers.

They come in all shapes, sizes and exist at all levels. They could be executives, department heads, administrative assistants, high-potentials or the savvy old-timers.

To find them, ask yourself: Who is highly respected by everyone? Who has the last word in discussions? Who gets the most air time, attention or validation in meetings? Who gets access to the resources, inside information, rumors and opportunities before anyone else?

Once you've identified these power figures, think through ways you can support their success. For example:

If an influential department head is looking for an HR volunteer for a productivity improvement task force, step forward.

If a highly-regarded colleague wants your insight about an executive you've worked with successfully, provide your best advice.

If your boss' admin is frustrated trying to find that ideal birthday gift for your boss, volunteer to help her find one.

The goal is to look for ways you can provide favors...both little ones and big ones.

Know Thy Enemies!

You will have your detractors.

With them, it's important that you rise above petty little personal conflicts and never, <u>ever</u> rely on their confidentiality. You don't have to be paranoid about this, but assume that anything you say to them will be gossiped about, shared or used to your disadvantage.

However, they are often difficult to spot. While some adversarial co-workers will confront you without hesitation, others operate under the radar.

In fact, your haters may not say anything to you at all, but use subtle little non-verbal cues like eye rolling, deep sighs or finger tapping while you're speaking. Or undermine you behind your back.

If it takes places in front of other people, diffuse the situation with a little light humor directed at the person in question.

If it happens more often, then confront the offender behind closed doors.

But pick your battles. While these behaviors may be distracting, you don't have to address every single one and they don't have to intimidate you.

Don't Take Sides In A Power Struggle!

In office politics, it is possible to find yourself stuck in between two big shots – with huge egos – who are constantly at odds.

This happened to me, years ago, when I had a dual reporting relationship to a powerful General Manager and our divisional head of HR at PepsiCo. Both of them hated each other.

I had the pleasure of being in the middle of their little tug of war while they tried consistently to outwit each other and defend their own turf on different HR issues.

In cases like this, after getting my head bashed in a few times, I learned the hard way that it was important to focus on "what was best for the business" and not take sides with either of them – even though I clearly liked one better than the other.

This strategy helped me remain above the fray and handle their conflict in an objective manner. It also helped me build trust with both parties. I've never forgotten the lesson.

Walk Your Own Talk!

Gaining a reputation as a person who is honest and dependable are qualities of the true office politician.

Do what you say you will do.

Stand up for the right things.

Practice what you preach.

Years ago, at a meeting of our African American Council at our division of Pepsi, the leaders were complaining that the company's progress on racial inclusion wasn't moving fast enough. Our executive sponsor, who was the white male CFO in the company, asked us out of curiosity to share the names of three people we were all personally mentoring. A few had none. Most had at least one. With a couple of exceptions, all the mentees named were the exact race and gender as we were.

He then challenged us by saying: "Guys, it's easy to whine. But as the senior African American leaders in this company, you're not walking the talk either. There's no way things will change if you're only mentoring people just like you. Here's what I'd propose. Why don't you set a personal objective for yourself that you will mentor 3 people over the next six months who are all different (more diverse than you are)? And I'll do the same thing, because frankly I need to walk the talk better too."

At a meeting six months later, we all excitedly reported back on our progress. Doing this was so insightful for us personally that we continued our mentoring relationships past the six months we had committed to. In addition, we all cascaded this down to our teams. This tiny effort soon spread throughout the company and gained lots of attention and support.

The lesson: whining got us nowhere. Walking our own talk did. And it helped us "politically" drive our diversity & inclusion initiative in the direction we wanted.

Think Win-Win!

Learn to think in terms of "**how can we <u>both</u> win in this situation?**"

This requires that you first understand the other party's perspective and what's in it for them. Next, understand what's in it for you. Then, strive to seek out a resolution that is acceptable and beneficial to both of you.

People simply don't like to lose. You may screw people over with win-lose tactics once or twice, but very soon, you'll find yourself without any allies at work.

Thinking win-win is a powerful and enduring strategy that builds relationships and helps you win in the long term.

Finally, Get A Mentor!

If you're not still not sure how to crack your company's political code *(and every company has one)* identify someone who seems especially comfortable building coalitions and is well-networked within your organization.

Then pick their brain to find out how they approach things.

I can almost guarantee the person

will be flattered and eager to help.

And you'll gain another ally that will support your success.

To Conclude...

The more relationships you nurture at work, the more you will get done and the more fun your work life will be.

Don't hate the game of politics.

Play it to win—but play it authentically and honorably.

If you don't know how to play, learn.

Remember, it's just folks interacting, building alliances and helping each other win.

Build Your HR Credibility From Day One!

There is an old story that circulated around the Quaker Oats Company in HR for years.

It's illustrates ONE important point about getting off to a great start as the new kid on block in HR.

It seems that two weeks after she arrived, the brand new Chief Human Resources Officer (CHRO) of a big Quaker Oats division was invited by the sales organization to be a featured guest speaker at their meeting at the corporate headquarters.

It would be the first time they would meet her in person.

Over breakfast with the group, she sat at the head table and said to the waiter, "Bring me another bowl of oatmeal."

The waiter says: "Can't. We're running out of oatmeal, so only one bowl of oatmeal per person."

"Do you know who I am?" asks the frustrated CHRO.

"Nope," says the waiter. "Who are you?"

"I'm the new head of HR for this division of Quaker Oats. I'm the featured guest speaker for their sales meeting. After breakfast, I'm going to share my wisdom with all these people around this table. That's who I am. And, now, I want another bowl of oatmeal."

"Well," says the waiter, "do you know who I am?"

"No," confessed the new HR chief.

The waiter smiled triumphantly. "I'm Quaker's head of cafeteria services and today, the man in charge of the oatmeal!"

Checkmate. Game over. End of discussion.

In attempting to establish yourself in HR from day one, it's easy to make the wrong assumptions. Or as in this case, fail to get to know the key people, be dismissive, step on toes, or create horrible first impressions even before you get started.

According to *HR Executive* magazine, nearly 50% of all new HR leaders — whether they are new HR managers or experienced directors or VPs — fall flat on their faces and fail in their first 18 months.

And, often, that failure is the result of crucial mistakes and missteps they make in the first 30 days — blunders that end up tripping up them up from the start. And, since mistakes made so early can be devastating, how do you avoid them?

I'm convinced that super-successful new Human Resources leaders find a way. They don't waste any time getting up to speed when they change jobs. They recognize the first 30 days is the best time to begin building relationships and establishing a platform for success during their "honeymoon" period so that they can make a big splash later on.

It's easy to screw up in your first 30 days, if you don't have a roadmap. So, in this chapter, I'd like to give you one.

I call it…

Your 30-Day Game Plan For Getting Off To A FAST START As A New HR Leader At Any Level & In Any Organization!

Begin By Meeting With Your Boss And Key Stakeholders A Few Times, Either In Person Or By Phone, <u>BEFORE</u> You Officially Take The Helm Of Your New Team!

Do this before arriving and you'll lay a great foundation for your first day. Use this time to gain clarity from your manager about your mission, goals, and objectives of the Company or the division or client group you are joining. Establish from her how you and your new HR team fit into the overall company....and what the 30 day, 90 day, 6 month and one year expectations are.

Example: Deon came into our organization as the new HR director for our Gatorade division. Her clients included seven plant managers – four of whom she talked with during her interviews. A week before she started she still had not met three of them. Anticipating a problem, I indicated to her that, politically, it was essential that she connect with ALL of them. *(We wanted no one feeling left out and holding it against her even before she had a chance to get out of the starting gate.)*

She immediately called each of them that week, introduced herself personally and expressed her enthusiasm about meeting them in person soon. Her clients were blown away by her desire to build relationships and work with them even before her official Day One.

As a result, when she arrived, she had already established positive "first impressions" and laid the groundwork with her key clients. And it got her off to a productively fast start.

Don't Wait. No Matter What Anyone Tells You, Hold A "GET ACQUAINTED" Staff Meeting On Your First Day As The New HR Leader!

Your new team will understandably be concerned about what the new boss is will be like, so don't keep them waiting and wondering.

You want to use this first staff meeting to express your enthusiasm and optimism to your team about your new HR role.

Many would have already googled you or scrutinized your professional profile on LinkedIn, so don't be surprised by that.

Just be prepared to answer any questions that your online information will likely prompt. Freely disclose your work history, your family background, spare time interests, your values and what's important to you.

Let them get to know the real, genuine, authentic you. You'll want to break the ice with them, so have each member of your new team do the same thing. Then briefly discuss your overall leadership style, how you plan to approach your new role and any initial expectations you have. _Make_ _this_ _all_ _positive._

If some members of your team are located out of town, include them in this first meeting as well -- in person, by video conference, by teleconference, skype or any other means. You want everyone to hear the same message from you on day one to minimize rumors or misunderstandings.

These early meetings will give everyone a chance to check you out at the same time.

But here's the REAL truth: Most will remember little about your first day beyond "hello."

That is, unless you screw up royally and say something you wish you'd never said.

Otherwise, just being open, personable and positive in your first brief team meeting on your first day will score you major early points with your team.

Use Your 30-Day "Honeymoon Period" To Go To School On Your New Team By Getting Brutally Candid Feedback About Them!

Talk to your boss about each person's past performance. Get copies of past performance reviews, 360 assessments, special recognition awards or other documents that speak to their current performance and future potential.

You want to determine who is great and who's not. You'll also want to gain a deep understanding of the history of the team. You'll also want to verify your initial assumptions about the team's capabilities with your clients as well.

Objectivity here is important, so be careful not to be biased by perceptions that cannot be supported with examples.

If Possible, Follow Up With Your Predecessor Before They Completely Check Out!

I can't tell you how many people fail to schedule overlap meetings with their predecessor.

Don't let your EGO get in the way. The person who has preceded you in your new HR role has information that can help you. So let them.

Use this as an opportunity to absorb their wisdom. If that person is leaving the company voluntarily with a good track record, it's well worth it to contact them in advance of your first day. If the person is remaining with the organization, that's even better. In either case you'll want to get their insight about:

(a) The history of the group you're inheriting

(b) Your new clients and their priorities

(c) List of the team's current and upcoming priorities

(d) Strengths, weaknesses, opportunities of your team

(e) Important contacts and resources

Again, this is your team now, so don't feel obligated to use everything that is offered.

And, if need be, get your new boss's help in lining up a discussion with your predecessor. It's that important.

Resist The Urge To Prove Yourself In The First Couple Of Weeks!

Take the time to learn about the new organization <u>first</u> before making major decisions.

Use your 30-day "honeymoon" period to absorb all you can about the products, the people, and the problems.

Probe to dig out deep insights from your clients, staff and colleagues about the HR issues and opportunities -- before deciding which major decisions and reforms to tackle.

Example: Rhonda didn't follow this advice. Rather, she chose to enter her new job as senior HR manager in Quaker's Food Service organization like a bull in a china shop.

She had just been promoted into this highly visible role and was anxious to prove herself.

Things ended quickly for her when she started making major changes in the college recruiting process, within her first month on the job, without engaging her stakeholders.

In fact, she never paused to build relationships with any of her colleagues, clients and contacts in other departments.

She just focused primarily on pleasing her boss.

So when he transferred to another division a few months after her arrival, Rhonda was left with NO other allies or supporters in the organization.

And, without this kind of support system, she didn't have a snowball's chance and was "excused" from the company after one year.

Stop Talking About Your Former Company!

No one wants to constantly hear you say, *"Well, at my old company, we did it this way...."* This not only sounds like your previous company did everything better, but also makes it appear that you miss your old job and aren't happy with the new one.

It's easy to fall into this trap. If you're leaving a mammoth organization like a Pepsi, General Electric or P&G, you can struggle if you're joining a much smaller organization.

The bigger companies are typically staffed with more resources and experts who can provide specialized help. For example, they have compensation specialists, employee benefits pros or labor relations gurus that you can draw on to deal with highly technical or legal HR issues. Not having this kind of in-house support at smaller firms can be hard to accept at first.

But, your focus should be forward, not backward. Talking about the way you did things at your previous company implies that your head or heart is still there. People will get sick of this quickly.

So don't do it.

Nobody cares.

Anticipate And Accept The Fact That You're Not Going To Be Everyone's BFF!

Don't expect to win popularity contests in your early days in your new role.

If you do, that's great. But don't plan on it. In no walk of life does everyone embrace the people making the decisions. This is especially true when you're the new HR leader.

When you start in a new company

or a different department within your existing organization, initially you would think that people would welcome you with open arms.

But often, it's with clinched fists.

There are always two groups of people. One group that will bond with you easily. The other group that will think: "Okay, another newbie. Let's see what's he or she is made of." And no matter what you do, it will take you time to win their support.

So how do you combat that?

Accept it!

No matter how good your credentials are, when you take on a new job, your reputation doesn't automatically arrive with you, no matter how great you are. With some people, you'll need to earn their acceptance.

Soothe Any "Ruffled Feathers" That May Exist If You Were Brought Into Your New HR Role Above Someone Who Thought They Should Have Had Your Job!

Often there are people who feel passed over for the job you've just filled.

A few of them may even be on your team.

To help cushion the impact of your arrival, ask your boss to reconcile any issues beforehand. Or make sure you and your role are positioned properly by that boss in order to minimize friction and discomfort, which will inevitably exist.

Once you arrive, don't waste time trying to discuss this delicate matter directly with these individuals, unless they bring it up first.

Instead, *by your actions*, indicate your desire to sincerely support and work successfully with these people…whether they want to not.

To Gain Clarity On Your New Accountabilities, Get The Org Charts...But DON'T Rely On Them!

While the organization chart may show you reporting to a single manager, often that's misleading.

Jobs change. Matrix organizations are alive and well in many large, globally complex organizations. You may have a strong dotted-line reporting relationship to another client you weren't aware of. Or you may have accountabilities or expectations from your boss that weren't clarified in the interview process. Or there may be clients or locations where you may "share" accountabilities with other HR leaders.

Often reporting relationships may not be as entirely clear or straightforward as depicted in the org chart.

So, review the organization charts in detail with your boss and go very deep to determine: (a) What your client locations or functions do, (b) How they do it, (c) What their HR expectations are of you and your team and (d) Your relationship with the rest of the HR organization.

Example: Ian was hired as a Compensation Director for a major division of an oil company. With his manager's help, he reviewed the org charts, charted out his key stakeholders and begun building relationships with them.

However, shortly thereafter, the Compensation Director of a different division began undermining Ian's work with the Corporate Compensation group -- a department that they both reported to on a dotted line basis.

Ian did not understand why his cross-divisional counterpart was working against him, since he had never met her.

It turned out she was miffed that he hadn't seen her as important enough to call or establish a relationship with. Previously, she had bonded well with his predecessor, enjoying their weekly chats about compensation policy and company gossip. She had hoped to establish the same relationship with Ian...*except no one told him.* Instead, unknowingly, he overlooked her when he compiled his list of key stakeholders to connect with. She saw this as a sign of disrespect and Ian created an unwarranted rift with her that took him months to resolve.

Find Out From Your Clients How Your HR Team Is Perceived And How Well It's Servicing The Organization!

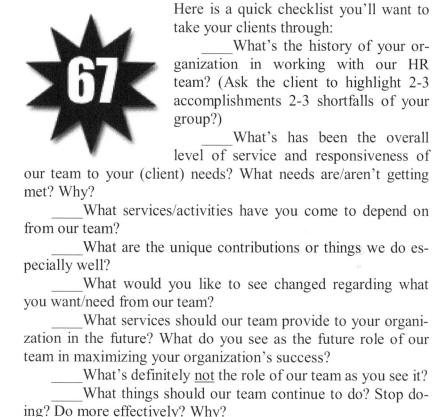

Here is a quick checklist you'll want to take your clients through:

_____What's the history of your organization in working with our HR team? (Ask the client to highlight 2-3 accomplishments 2-3 shortfalls of your group?)

_____What's has been the overall level of service and responsiveness of our team to your (client) needs? What needs are/aren't getting met? Why?

_____What services/activities have you come to depend on from our team?

_____What are the unique contributions or things we do especially well?

_____What would you like to see changed regarding what you want/need from our team?

_____What services should our team provide to your organization in the future? What do you see as the future role of our team in maximizing your organization's success?

_____What's definitely not the role of our team as you see it?

_____What things should our team continue to do? Stop doing? Do more effectively? Why?

_____If you could wish for anything from our team, what would you wish for?

_____If we could provide all the things you might wish for, what things would you value most? (Prioritize the wish list).

_____How can I ensure there's good on-going communications between your organization and my team? (e.g., How will I find out if it's not going well? Or if everything is okay?)

Asking the "stop-start-and-continue" question in this checklist is critical. From this very simple question, you'll get answers back like, *"I'd like faster turnaround time on compensation decisions"* or *"We need to move faster on developing the leadership development program I discussed with your boss a month ago!"*

Finally, let your clients know that you've heard them and share what specific actions you'll be taking based on their comments. Also indicate that going forward you'd like to continue to get this kind of regular feedback on a regular basis.

As You Discuss New Performance Expectations With Each Member of Your New Team, Look For Early Opportunities To Give Credit And Recognition For What They've Done Well In The Past!

Clearly you'll want to renegotiate your staff's performance objectives so everyone knows what you expect and how their performance ties to what you're trying to achieve

However, no one likes to think that their accomplishments before your arrival were worthless and in vain.

So be prepared to give credit and mucho respect to the members of your team. Seek out their opinions. Listen to their ideas. Develop your staff as a group of allies. Involve them in key decisions and let them guide and help you through your initial period of taking charge, until you get more comfortable in your new role.

Example: Dick fell flat on his face when we hired him as the new HR leader of our Foods division – primarily because he disrespected his new team.

Armed with mandate to "take his new HR organization to the next level," he refused to acknowledge the great relationships his team had already established with their clients. He also arrogantly dismissed and discounted their great performance results, which weren't done in his watch.

As a result, he never won them over. And when his two top direct reports resigned in frustration for "better opportunities," it got worse. He told the remaining team members to pick up the slack, while continuing to withhold much-needed praise and recognition from them. His inconsiderate actions caused the team's morale and performance to drop further. To no one's surprise, Dick was fired after his first performance review.

"Buddy" Up With A Peer Or Seasoned Colleague Who Can Help You Decipher The Culture!

Many large organizations have complex cultures that are tough to figure out. And making assumptions or executing HR initiatives without assessing their "cultural fit" first can lead to painful and embarrassing mistakes later.

Don't fall in this trap. Buddy up with a peer or a seasoned colleague who can coach you on the culture.

Utilize this new "buddy" to provide you with insights on how the formal and informal systems in the organization work.

You can also utilize him or her to introduce and connect you with others in the organization you can later use as a support system to draw on to ask questions, be a sounding board and provide additional insights about the organization.

Invest as much time learning the climate and culture of the organization as you do developing your knowledge of the business and their specific HR practices.

Knowing what to do is not enough. You must also know how to work within the personality and fabric of the company.

Assess The Landscape First, Before Making Your Contributions in Meetings!

It's obviously important that you make your impact visible in key meetings.

But you will want to first observe and pay careful attention to meeting dynamics, the style of how information is presented and decisions are made.

Who are the strong players?

Who gets deferred to?

Who are the real influencers?

Are meetings formal or informal?

Do decisions really get made in meetings or are they dog and ponies, with the <u>real</u> decisions made elsewhere?

Are power point presentations the norm...or handouts used...or has the organization gone totally "green" and operates paperless?

These are just a few areas you'll want to assess before diving head first into the meeting waters.

Identify 2-3 Areas Where You Can Initiate HR Reforms To Get Some "Early Wins!"

Once you've done what has been suggested so far, still resist the temptation to make everything happen all at once in your first month. You don't have to go for a home-run in your early decisions.

Just focus your group's energy on a "short list" of 2-3 carefully chosen projects that will provide some early successes and impact within the organization.

The projects you choose should clearly address the biggest "pain points" that you've heard from your clients. While these initiatives may take longer than 30 days to complete, you should aim to identify them within your first month.

With Your Direct Reports And Clients, Identify Something You Can Bring To The Party That Adds Value In Their Eyes!

With your team, develop a **rallying cry, theme,** or **challenge** to unite the group.

Team members expect that a new HR leader will come up with something that will guide the team and clarify priorities going forward. Whether that something is called a "vision," "mission" or "purpose"…or simply a "new direction" is immaterial.

What is important is that you clarify where you see the team headed in the future. This direction should describe where your team needs to get and how it should work together to get there.

And, in the early stages of developing it, it's critical to involve the key members of your team in defining it. This may require holding many, many discussions early on. But in the end, it ensures that your direction is something your team members can get inspired and excited about.

After The First 2-3 Weeks, Start Soliciting Personal Feedback From Your Boss!

You'll probably get feedback well before this time, but just in case you don't, you want to convey that you're open to input and suggestions.

You will especially want to find out if there are early issues with the "fit" of your personal style with the culture of the organization.

First impressions would have had a chance to begin to take root and early impression formed. Be prepared to flex your style and recognize there are different ways to get things done.

Finally, After 30 Days
Start Keeping A "Success" File!

If you follow just half of the previous suggestions in your first month, you will have launched yourself well and established a strong foundation for your next 6-12 months.

With that in mind, I have ONE final suggestion: Begin compiling a file containing your "successes."

Why? Because being a brand new HR leader can be a lonely proposition filled with discouragement, setbacks and frustrations. Occasionally you'll have dark days when you will question yourself and you'll wonder if it's all worth it. That's when you want to pull out this file containing all the letters, accolades and positive e-mails you've received from your clients, your boss, your team and others whose viewpoints matter.

Read through them. Then get back to work.

It will give you a boost.

Try it: Use it sparingly – don't get lost in past glory – but keep it around for when you need that coffee-free lift.

To conclude...

One of these days you'll transition into a new HR leadership role and you'll want some proven guidance on how to hit the ground fast. You now have it. So bookmark this chapter and file it away for the future. Or better yet, share it with a colleague or one of your direct reports. I'm sure they'll appreciate the help.

Sell Your HR Ideas!

Without This ONE Indispensable Skill, You Will Never, Ever Win Big in HR...

In every HR job I've ever had, I spent 90% of my time doing one thing. And that one thing was...**SELLING!**

- **When I recruited MBA candidates on campus, I was eagerly SELLING them on why my company was better than our competition.**

- In labor negotiations, I was passionately SELLING our union leaders on why they should give concessions in the collective bargaining agreement to help the organization.

- **When I was pitching my latest and greatest new fangled HR idea, I was doing some serious SELLING to our executives on why they should invest the company's hard-earned dollars in my little thingy versus someone else's.**

- In exit interviews with talent we wanted to retain, I was desperately SELLING them on why they should reconsider and stay with the company…even though I knew by then was too late and there wasn't a snowball's chance of it happening.
- **In new employee orientation programs, I was enthusiastically SELLING newbies on why joining our company was the best thing for their career, for their family, for their life.**
- When reviewing resumes with our hiring managers, I was SELLING them on why a particular candidate was a superstar and worthy of an hour of their time for an exploratory look-see.
- **When budgets were frozen, I was doing fact-based SELLING to the CFO on why we should pay our top people more this year if we wanted to stay competitive within our market.**
- I was SELLING headhunters, university professors and placement directors and faculty influencers on why they should push the best candidates in our direction.
- **I was SELLING executives on why we needed to invest more in HR technology to streamline our performance management and career development systems.**
- In meetings, telephone conversations, hallway showdowns, cafeteria handshakes, parking lot discussions, text messages…and even awkward bathroom situations, I was…

SELLING. SELLING. SELLING.

Many times, I felt like a used car salesman moving through the hallways and elevators at PepsiCo.

Many nights when I got home from work, dead tired, I felt as if I'd been running for political office all day.

But I understood…my major job was selling.

And if you're in HR, guess what?

THAT'S A <u>HUGE</u> PART OF YOUR JOB TOO!

Without the ability to SELL, influence and persuade your career in HR is dog poo…and you will forever be relegated to the back of the kennel. Not at the front where the "show dogs" sit.

All great HR executives and professionals are great salespeople. And they recognize that getting others to support your ideas and follow your direction is a critical HR skill.

But there are requirements for being a good salesperson in HR.

It requires that you ABSOLUTELY, TOTALLY BUY-IN and are PASSIONATE about what you're selling.

It requires that you know how to build relationships, listen, position your ideas, handle resistance, explore alternatives, and get agreement.

It also requires an iron spine to handle resistance and rejection.

Like any salesperson, you'll hear the word "no."

Often.

You'll get the door slammed in your face.

Often.

Sometimes it will happen loudly.

And sometimes you will be rejected so subtly you won't realize until later that you were rebuffed -- by someone who was BETTER at the game of selling than you were!

But that's okay.

Learn from them.

And begin positioning these "no's" in your mind as challenges, not as rejections. And then figure out what you'll do next.

So, if you already know how to sell, that's terrific.

If you don't, learn.

How? To start, kindle or pick up *Yes!* by Robert Cialdini or *Flawless Consulting* by Peter Block. Get some coaching by someone you consider to be an expert in your organization.

Then keep growing and building this skill.

It's one of the best investments you will ever make in your career.

Win Over Your CEO!

The CEO Put A Gun To My Head.
How I Survived & You Can Too!

A few years ago, I was scheduled to give a one hour presentation to the PepsiCo CEO and her senior leadership team.

The purpose of my presentation was to get their approval for three new HR programs. These programs would start in one division and then expand across all divisions in the company and cost $7 million. So I needed to get buy-in from the CEO and her division heads. And, they would all be there in the meeting.

Because of overloaded travel schedules and other priorities, it had taken four months for me to get my presentation on their agenda.

Needless to say, I was excited and just a little nervous about getting in front of the top brass.

I planned on presenting for 40 minutes – not a full hour — to leave enough time for Q&A at the end.

When the day finally came, I traveled from Chicago to the PepsiCo HQ in New York. I arrived an hour before my presentation, checked in with the receptionist and sat in the waiting room just outside the board room.

I had my game face on and told myself that I couldn't be more ready.

In the weeks leading up to the presentation, I'd rehearsed in front of my boss, my team, my bathroom mirror, Peppi (my dog) and anyone else I could find.

I had practiced handling just about any objection they could possibly toss my way. Every chart, graph and data point on my power point slides had been carefully researched, scrubbed, debated and double-checked to make sure it was precise. I worked out all the bugs. The presentation was tight and ready to go.

Not only was I prepared, I had over-prepared. But as prepared as I was…I WASN'T READY FOR WHAT HAPPENED NEXT!

As I sat in the waiting room ready to go in, the time finally arrived for my presentation. But they were not ready for me yet. They were still in the meeting room, door closed. So I waited. 30 minutes went by. Then 60 minutes. Then 90 minutes. Then two hours. While I anxiously waited, the CEO's executive assistant looked in on me, assuring me that I had not been forgotten and to be patient.

Finally…after 2 1/2 hours past the original time of my presentation, the door to the board room opened.

The CEO was the first person to come out. She immediately rushed over to me and said, "Alan, I really apologize that we're running so far behind time. We're going to take a 15 minute break now. I know you came all the way from Chicago, and that we promised you an hour but unfortunately, we can only give you 10 minutes to present. It's our fault. Is that enough time or would you like us to reschedule you?" *Though she spoke very politely, it was clear from her focused facial expression that lobbying her for more time was not an option for me.*

Totally caught off-guard, I felt like…

The CEO had just put a gun to my head!

She was only going to give me 10 minutes for a presentation originally scheduled for an hour.

And in my mind, I thought: "Jeez, it had taken 4 months to get on the schedule in the first place, now they're running behind…and there was no telling how long it would take for me to get time with this group again. And what if I refuse her offer to present now? Have I just killed my career in HR?"

Thinking quickly under this pressure and finally concluding that I didn't want to waste this opportunity, I responded: "Sure, I understand fully. If we only have 10 minutes, I'll make it work."

Here's what I then did.

During that 15 minute break, I took my 16 power point slides (and my 60 back up slides)…and immediately trashed all but 4 of them!

Then I went into the board room during the break and found the AV guy who was setting up all the presentations and told him which slides I was going to use.

After that, I tried to compose myself. If I was a little nervous before, with this curve ball, I was now in a full-scale panic. But I refused to give in to it. Instead, I headed for the men's room to get myself psyched back up. I wasn't going let this last minute change in plan throw me off my game.

While in the john, I went over my opening remarks again. I had to mentally shorten my intro since my time had now been cut by 75%. I then exhaled and went back in the board room.

When I got up to present, to my surprise, everything just flowed. My nervousness went away in about 10 seconds. I enjoyed myself. I went through my four slides in 10 minutes.

And then I was promptly hit with 30 minutes of questions from the group! Tough ones. Easy ones. But no surprises. Overall, the Q&A was freewheeling, wide-ranging and often got off-topic.

Wow! I could see why these guys were behind schedule!

Finally, after 40 minutes — not the 10 minutes I expected — the CEO cut off the discussion and with the support of the team gave her approval for all three of my HR programs and the budget I wanted.

I left the meeting a happy camper.

The next day, I got a nice thank you note from her with a copy to my boss.

Sweet.

And, needless to say, all of this helped me tremendously when performance reviews rolled around a few months later.

However, besides getting the go-ahead for my HR programs, I learned some important lessons from that traumatic experience that were even more valuable.

Here they are…

12 Tips For Winning Big When Presenting To The CEO & Other Senior Higher Ups!

Give Yourself Permission To BE The Expert!

Yes, you are meeting with the high ranking person in your organization. However, CEOs are not experts in every single specialized area of the company.

Typically, they have 12-16 hour days where they are in back-to-back meetings ALL day, every day. Each meeting has a vastly different topic. In the eyes of each person that meets with them, it's the most important priority in the world. And they are expected to give the CEO enough information, data and perspective to enable a high level decision to be made.

That's day of a typical CEO.

So it's YOUR job, to be their expert in your area.

They expect nothing less.

If you aren't ready to demonstrate that, you have no reason to meet with them.

Cut To The Chase!

When presenting to the CEO and/or the top management team, forget the formalities.

Cut the crap and dive right into what you want to say and what they need to know. Nothing more.

Senior teams are impatient, hear dozens of presentations every week and have short attention spans.

Drop the opening pleasantries ("I'm happy to be here with you today").

If your time on the agenda has been cut, don't make excuses, apologize or explain how or why your time is limited. Just begin!

Know Your Opening Cold!

If you're going to screw up, chances are it will happen in your opening remarks.

And messing up the opening can throw you off, and destroy your confidence and before you know it, you're drooling all over yourself.

So make sure you know your opening like the back of your hand.

After you speak your first words, you'll relax. And when you relax, the rest of your presentation will just flow.

For example, begin by saying something like: *"Good morning, I'm here today to get your approval for a new employee benefit program that will save us $2 million in health care costs and improve our retention by 7%."*

That's it. It grabs their attention and is short, sharp and too-the-point.

When in doubt, keep in mind the phrase: *"Be brief, Be bright and then Be gone!"*

Use Only 3
Main Supporting Points!

Don't overload your presentation minor facts, statistics or "nice to know" info.

Pick your three strongest points and present only as much fact-based data and supporting statements as the execs need to know in order to agree with you.

Also eliminate fluff and slides that don't advance your message – like the cover slide, the agenda slide and transition slides.

If in doubt about certain slides, keep them on hand as back-ups to use during the Q&A...if you get the chance.

As Important As Your
Presentation Is, Q&A Is
Even More Important!

You can do a great job of presenting but it can all fall apart when the time comes for questions.

Failure to respond to questions well can undermine any credibility you've built while giving your presentation.

The key here is not to take questions – even aggressive questions — personally.

This is not an indictment of you.

Just consider tough questions like all the others, simply requests for information in order for the questioner to better understand what you're presenting.

Man Up!
Be Decisive and Fact-Based!

Avoid the temptation to say "I think this" or "I feel that."

Instead say: "Here's what we need to do and here are the facts and data to back it up."

The senior group wants to see and feel that you're supremely confident about what you're proposing.

Any hesitation or a lack of substantiation for your idea will make you look unprepared, unprofessional and not ready for prime time.

Long before you make your pitch, make sure you fact-check any claims you'll be making.

If there are opinions you have that won't stand up to a challenge, either go back and build a case for them or take them out of your presentation entirely.

Be Ready For Curveballs
And If Necessary Throw Away Your Script!

You can be pissed off, exasperated and irritated when you've been thrown a curveball, but you shouldn't be surprised by them.

Just because you're prepared to present a certain way doesn't mean you'll get to do it exactly the way you planned.

Senior leaders have their own agenda, and sometimes you have to be ready to flex yours for theirs. If they want your presentation to go in a different order or even a different direction from what you planned, you should be ready to adjust. What's the point of insisting on your agenda, only to have your words land on a tuned-out audience? If you've rehearsed, if you've anticipated what your audience might ask, you'll be in a good position to be flexible, fast on your feet, and ready to improvise.

Prepare Like You Would For A Job Interview!

Learn everything you can about your CEO (and any others in the room) ahead of time.

Read the information provided on your company website – often found under "About" or "For Investors." Do a Google search, including recent news, in order to get an external perspective. Read through any recent speeches. Talk to others that know the CEO and have had meetings with him or her. You may not end up using any of this information, but it will make you feel much more prepared and comfortable. And who knows, there may be an opportunity to make a personal connection or informed comment…or to at least avoid putting your foot in your mouth.

Rehearse, Rehearse, Rehearse!

Everyone can't think as well on their feet as Tony Robbins or other professional speaking gurus. I certainly can't.

And, it's a rare person who can wing it and do well. So you must prepare. Even the pros who give speeches for a living invest hours in practice time behind closed doors. So if you want to come across naturally, make sure you take time to prepare. Rehearse the Q&A. Anticipate every question. Practice your answers. Write them all out. If you do that, even if you're asked a question you didn't expect, you'll find that a great answer will emerge from everything you anticipated.

Be Clear On What Would Be a "WIN!"

Ask yourself what you'd like to achieve as a result of this meeting?

Are you looking for approval, and if so, is that a reasonable expectation? Or are you looking for interest and a definitive next step? Being clear and realistic on what would be your "win" will increase your chances of getting it.

End Early If You Can!

If you've achieved your win, and there's still 10 minutes left, close your presentation and offer to give that 10 minutes back to the CEO.

They'll either thank-you or invite you to stay. Either way, they will appreciate the gesture, as will the next person waiting outside for their turn.

End by thanking them for their time and thank their Executive Assistant on the way out.

Own The Follow-Up!

A wise mentor once told me "never leave the CEO or a senior executive with a long to-do list."

For one thing, it may not get done.

But more importantly, the CEO will greatly value your respect for their time and your willingness and ability to get things done on his/her behalf.

After the meeting, send a brief thank-you, meeting summary, including any decisions and next steps.

Then exhale.

The Sneaky, Little Secret For Getting Buy-In To Your HR Ideas That Almost Never Fails!

When the PepsiCo CEO put a gun to my head – things worked out in the end and I got out of there my "win."

However, if I'm honest with myself, I could have prepared better. There's one tactic I didn't use in my prep that could have improved my chances for success TEN-FOLD.

This one, single tactic is shockingly simple.

It is more important than how **innovative** your HR idea is. It is more important than **how many dollars** your HR idea can deliver to your company's bottom line.

That's how important this ONE single idea is.

But, enough suspense. Let me spill the beans and tell you what this is all about.

It involves ensuring that there are NO SHOCKING REVELATIONS or SURPRISES for your key decision makers when the time comes for them to finally approve your HR idea.

And there's only one way this can happen. And you should inscribe this in your mind, forever. Here it is…

You must <u>pre-wire</u> your HR ideas!

Pre-wiring involves taking key decision-makers through the key elements in your proposal early...long before you gather them together in a conference room to go through your final pitch for approval. You want them already bought-in **before the time finally comes for them to officially say "YES."**

Often resistance to your big, new or innovative HR idea occurs NOT because it isn't good. But, because some of the decision makers didn't have enough time (or advance warning) to get comfortable with it.

And to protect themselves from approving something they aren't ready for, they'll either:

- Cross-examine you with so many questions you'll feel like a serial killer on trial.
- Delay making a decision until you provide them with more data…lots of it.
- Make excuses that this just isn't the right time to do it.
- Or, they'll just flat out trash or reject your idea.

All of which will make you feel that just you've dealt with a bunch of nitpickers, naysayers and handwringers.

So, before you do any kind of formal presentation with a large group to get buy-in, you'll want to do some pre-wiring beforehand. This will give your audience a chance to process your idea.

This can involve sending out a summary of your recommendations far in advance of their final decision, asking them for feedback and comments first. Or even better yet, if you can schedule some brief one-on-ones with a few of the key influencers in the group beforehand, your chances for success rise dramatically.

Most HR folks overlook the importance of doing this. But it has three benefits:

(1) It will keep you from **getting blindsided** by major objections when you finally present your ideas to the entire group.

(2) It will also help you **build a consensus** in favor of your ideas among those who have to approve or implement them, and

(3) It will give you a chance to **modify your ideas** to incorporate their input which can help better fit your idea to the political realities of your organization.

Pre-wiring is critical.

So the next time you are scheduled to sell your latest and greatest HR project to a bunch of decision-makers in a swanky conference room, ask yourself WHO do you need pre-wire in advance — and how will you do it?

Your answer to this question may well be YOUR key to successfully getting that project embraced, sold and implemented.

And, it may even enhance your HR career in the process.

Supersize Your Network!

Building Your Network of Contacts Is Essential For Winning Big in HR. Treat Every Gathering You Attend As An Opportunity To Grow Your Relationships!

Gatherings are important. It doesn't matter whether it is formally called a "networking event" or not – use it as a chance to expand and deepen your contact network.

This get-together could be any of the following:

- The monthly business meeting that everyone goes to.
- The annual HR meeting that includes your team and the other HR functions in your organization.
- The monthly local Society of Human Resources (SHRM) association meeting you attend regularly.
- A conference call you're on where everyone is discussing the pressing HR issue of the moment.

- A meet-up at the local bar where folks at the office hang out for beers on Friday after a rough week.
- Or even a quick get-together to celebrate someone's birthday at the office.

The best networking and relationship building opportunities occur in situations like these when you don't know everyone there.

In these types of venues, focus on briefly introducing yourself, engage in some brief small talk and then follow-up later – perhaps over a coffee or lunch.

Some HR pros make the common mistake of being in a rush and so they try to move the networking and relationship building process along too quickly.

For example, if you've asked someone to write down the names of job leads at their current company -- and you've just met them -- you've gone too fast. Big mistake.

That's like asking someone to marry you on the first date. You look desperate and foolish.

Avoid the high-pressure tactics - they aren't necessary.

Offer Your Help & Assistance – FIRST!

Dale Carnegie put it best:

"You can build more relationships in TWO MONTHS by becoming interested in other people than you can in TWO YEARS by trying to get people interested in you."

As you get to know people better, listen closely for opportunities where you can provide help. If someone you want to build a relationship with mentions they've had a rough time recruiting finance candidates, you might offer to send them the latest white paper on finance recruitment you've just come across. Or you might introduce them to a person you know who has a massive number of contacts in finance. These are all great ways to offer your help and assistance -- FIRST.

The key is listening closely and then generously sharing your talents, knowledge, and ideas. However, don't be disappointed if your generosity is not returned immediately.

Often, the "good karma" you've generated almost always yields benefits down the road – maybe not from this person – but from places and people you might not expect.

Every Day Compliment Someone – Either By Text, E-Mail Or In Person!

I mentioned this before in #8, but it's worth reiterating again, because it's just that important.

Pick out one of your contacts and comment on something they've done recently or well.

Be specific.

Speak from the heart.

Tell them why they rock.

It doesn't need to take much time – it can be a two or three sentence e-mail, text, voice mail message or in person.

Do one compliment a day and that's 365 compliments a year. The more strokes you give, the stronger your network can become.

It's a great way of re-connecting with someone you've not talked to in a while and it shoots you up their line of sight and top of mind…and your one minute of attention can potentially make their day.

Reach Out On LinkedIn And Recruit New Contacts!

Every time you check out your profile, LinkedIn recommends new people that you should follow. Reach out to one of these people each day and invite them to join your LI network. Focus on people in your region or city (Chicago, Cedar Rapids, etc.), in your discipline (HR executives, Talent Acquisition experts, Compensation folks, etc.) or just people you flat out find intriguing. Little by little you will find your network will grow using this <u>one</u> strategy alone.

While You're On LinkedIn, Take These Two Additional Actions!

Number one: Pick out someone to compliment.

Take time to read through list of updates provided on your profile by all your current contacts on LinkedIn.

Pick out one of their updates to comment on, acknowledge, congratulate or send a compliment to. Again, this helps strengthen that relationship.

Number two: Post a comment in your update box.

Do this every day.

Post something.

It's a way of letting people know you're still out there. Share a favorite quote, a link to great article or something you've experienced or learned that is of value to others…and it will get you into their head. Be positive. Be humorous. Be insightful. Prove that you're a thought leader and a subject matter expert, even if you aren't. Be shameless. Don't be petrified that you're saying the wrong thing…unless your name is Charlie

Sheen (then you should shoot yourself). All it takes is one sentence of 140 characters a day that adds value to others and you'll climb back on their radar screen.

The Unfortunate, Brutal Truth About The Relationships You Build In HR!

A few days ago, I had lunch with a good friend of mine who just landed a new job.

She will be heading up HR for the Canadian division of a new technology firm.

Needless to say, she's excited about her new gig. And I'm excited for her.

You see, we met as HR colleagues at Quaker Oats sixteen years ago and have been friends ever since. We've been there for each other through good times and bad — divorce, re-marriage, deaths in our family, raising kids, career disappointments, bad bosses, layoffs, illnesses, and job changes.

Even though she's moving to her new job in Toronto, and I'm in Chicago, I have no doubt that we'll keep in contact. I consider her a lifetime friend. And, I have very few people in my life that I consider LIFETIME friends. Friends, yes. Lifetime friends, no.

Thinking of her new role reminded me of all the HR jobs I've had. Over the years, I was always meeting new people, building relationships with many of them – and then leaving them or getting left behind when they moved on.

In cases where my working relationships developed into personal friendships, going our separate ways was never easy. At farewell parties, there were always tears, followed by sadness, and sometimes just a deep feeling of loss.

You each say you will keep in contact.

And you do. For awhile.

But then one day one of you just stops calling, e-mailing or texting.

There was no fight, no reason, you both just stopped.

Unfortunately, I've learned that many work relation-ships in HR come and go, but your life and your career goes on. Very few develop into deep, lifelong friendships. I know that sounds harsh.

But it's the brutal truth.

Your good friends will come and go....

Most people you meet in your life will just fade away.

Most of your high school friends won't be part of your college life.

Most of your college friends won't be a part of your 20-something professional life.

Most of your 20-something friends won't be there when...after many years of effort... you finally land that job of your dreams in HR.

But some friends will stick. And it is these friends – the ones who transcend time with you – who <u>DO</u> matter.

Cherish them.

And stay in touch.

Make Time For Big Work!

What Super-Busy HR People Do To Free Up Time So They Can Accomplish Awesome Stuff Faster!

Time is the most precious asset I have and it seems to run out constantly.

There never seems to be enough of it to allow me to do the BIG WORK in HR which is all about:

- Planning and creating new HR initiatives
- Solving major organization problems
- Or capitalizing on emerging strategic HR opportunities.

If I'm not careful, most of the day is spent busying myself with LITTLE WORK: bureaucratic or clerical tasks, unimportant meetings or reacting to minor issues others can handle.

There isn't a day that goes by I don't push something aside, and say to myself: "Boy, if I were able to squeeze in an extra hour to work on this, it would make a huge difference."

Not to make excuses, but there are many enemies stand in my way. I call them *time vampires*.

What are time vampires?

They are selfish, needy, and vicious creatures who want to suck up all my attention, energy and productivity.

They're absolutely everywhere. They're always on the attack. And, they're ruthless.

I confess that I'm not always 100% successful in dealing with them and it's a never ending battle. I've learned painfully that I can't give up, so I persist. However, I've discovered that the best way to protect myself from these blood-sucking creatures is to spot them and deal with them when they first appear.

So, if you're a super-busy HR pro, juggling a thousand different priorities and want to figure out how to accomplish the things that really matter…then, tune in.

Here are the five common time vampires and how to stop them in their tracks.

Stop "Mr. Gotta-Minute"

The most evil time vampire is Mr. Gotta-Minute.

He hides in the shadows outside your office or a few feet from the stall when you're in the john — just waiting to attack. When you least expect it, he pounces on you with: "Have you got a minute?" He has a knack of surprising you just when you are in middle of an urgent HR project or rehearsing for a crucial presentation to your higher ups.

He can be tough to resist. It seems easier to just deal with his "one quick question" now rather than later. You don't want to be rude. But guess what, he doesn't deserve your courtesy.

If you think about it, he's really dissing you by implying that his time is more valuable than yours and that what you're doing is unimportant and interruptible.

So go ahead and drive a stake through his heart with no remorse.

Here is how you stop him in his tracks: "I'm busy right now. Let's meet at 4:30 p.m. for 20 minutes and tackle everything on your list at that time."

Of course, this bloodthirsty vampire may not get it the first, or even the second or third time you do this.

But keep whipping out your stake every time, over and over again, eventually he'll get the message.

One day, he'll call you and say: "Hey, I've got these four things I need to go over with you. When can we get together?" After getting over your shock, congratulate yourself for having house-broken this particular vampire.

One BIG CAUTION before you use this strategy: In many organizations, it is expected that HR operate with an "open-door" and it's normal to have people interrupting you unexpectedly. So you should use this vampire-killing strategy selectively.

That is, "close your door" when you <u>absolutely</u> must focus.

And "open it" when you don't mind being interrupted.

But if you're busy constantly, let people know what your priorities are, so that your closed door is not <u>misinterpreted.</u>

However, if after providing explanations, your visitors don't understand, screw 'em! You have to make trade-offs and take strong positions when it comes to protecting your precious minutes. If you don't communicate and TRAIN PEOPLE on how to best utilize your time – it will absolutely be abused.

There's nothing wrong with creating "designated hours" to talk to people.

But permitting them to drop in unannounced all day long is NOT part of the HR job — <u>IF</u> they're taking you away from BIG work and critical organization priorities.

Kill Ms. Meeting-Itis

You know you've met Ms. Meeting-Itis when she drags you into a 30-minute meeting for the sole purpose of planning a much longer meeting.

She knows that for some HR people being in meetings is seductive. It's a way to feel important and a great way to hide from making decisions and taking responsibility for them. "Meeting-itis" is a disease that turns many HR pros into unproductive, slow-moving, indecisive drones.

Here's how to kill her: First, before you pull out your stake to go for her heart, push back and ask: "Do I really need to be in this meeting?" "Is there a more time-efficient way to handle this?" Or "Can I send an e-mail or voice-mail message to each meeting attendee before the meeting with my thoughts?"

If that doesn't work and you must attend a meeting called by this hell-bent, blood sucking animal, do this to get in and out fast: First, find out in advance what you're expected to contribute, then deliver it quickly in the meeting. Then, have an exit strategy. Get someone to come in to get you; or call your cell phone at a certain time. You can then excuse yourself to take the call, promising to return – but don't.

Drive Away Ms. Drama Queen

Everyone knows about drama queens. They turn every little issue into an emotional crisis.

She needs constant coddling. If you don't give her regular compliments about her work, she turns into a child who isn't getting enough hugs from Mommy. No matter how much you indulge her, she will always find a new way to soak up your precious time by pulling you into her drama by demanding that you give her reassurance, attention or a shoulder to cry on. Meanwhile, while she's resting their head on your shoulder, she's sticking her fangs into your neck and taking out a pint.

Here's the stake you use to drive this awful vampire away: Cut to the core of her problem and tell her what to do. This is exactly NOT what she wants. She doesn't want solutions, she wants an acting partner in her drama. If you refuse to play along, she'll likely look for new blood to drain elsewhere. Another option is to take over the conversation with a long, boring story of your own: "That reminds me of the story of what happened to old Uncle Ned during World War I..." In other words, turn into a vampire yourself and start sucking. She'll look for her own exit strategy.

Interrupt Mr. Trivia.

You know him. He's the guy who can't tell the difference between no-big-deal and a crisis.

He has a knack for pulling you away from your important tasks to deal with his own minor issues (i.e. The copy machine is stuck).

This is the stake you use: Interrupt this interrupter. Tell him something like, "I've got a lot on my plate today, so I will only be addressing issues that are a nine or ten on a one to ten scale. Everything else *must* wait until next week. Are you convinced that the issue you'd like to discuss is a nine or a ten?" Once you hear the word "no," leave. Leave, even if you're in your own office! By tomorrow, he'll likely have forgotten. And you'll live to work another day.

As with all vampires, your productivity increases by leaps and bounds as you get more skilled at spotting them and driving stakes through their hearts.

Embrace Dr. Sweat!

Jogging. Working out. Tennis. Biking. Lifting weights. Tread milling. Doing pilates.

Anything that makes you sweat is the way to combat the vampire called inactivity.

Physical exercise, of any kind whatsoever, followed by relaxation, will clear your mind and dramatically improve your personal productivity in HR.

Now for most of us, this is a blinding flash of the obvious.

Unfortunately, for others of us in HR, we treat exercise like it's a choice.

And that's a problem.

It reminds me of when e-mail first became widely used. I worked for a high-powered HR guy who thought doing e-mail was optional. He, like a lot of lofty executives at the time, liked to walk around bragging: "Call my secretary. I don't have email." It was like a badge of honor. I remember thinking that this guy didn't understand reality. Times had changed. His career was going to end if he couldn't manage to take a look in his e-mail box at least a couple of times a day.

Sure enough, that's what happened.

He thought he had a choice. So, he refused to embrace this change (and many others as well) and he quickly became a dinosaur. And, like all prehistoric creatures, he became extinct…and expendable.

Today, I believe the same is true about exercise…it is no longer optional. **It is now an essential part of building a successful career in HR.**

It's proven. Regular exercise changes your life and makes you more successful. Sure, it will also allow you attract more eyeballs at the beach or fit into your skinny jeans. But it goes deeper than that.

Mary Carmichael, a while back wrote in *Newsweek* about the research that shows exercise boosts our IQ and increases our resilience in tough times -- which is often the difference between success and failure in getting what we want in our life and in our career.

So to me, it's always been absurd to think that you can manage your time effectively without regular exercise. However, I didn't always practice what I knew to be true.

Recently, I re-learned this lesson when I started going to the gym again. Even though I knew better, I had gotten woefully out of shape. I had become overwhelmed by my HR work schedule and convinced myself that I didn't have time to fit in a daily workout.

However, I'd forgotten what all super-busy, high achieving HR people know....

Working out doesn't COST you time. Instead, it's an INVESTMENT of your time that pays dividends and improves your results.

Within two days of starting up my exercise program, after months of inactivity, I immediately began to reap the rewards. I have more energy. My mind is clearer. I seem to solve problems faster. I feel more confident and decisive. I'm finding that I'm more creative. I feel less overwhelmed.

And I don't have to invest in a new wardrobe (which is something I can now take off my to-do list).

However, making the transition from couch potato to regular exerciser isn't easy.

It requires a careful mental shift. You must clearly prioritize it at the top of your schedule. You must pick a specific time (I'm a morning guy) and specific place (I visit a fitness center nearby), and then convince yourself that doing it is NOT negotiable.

This means getting up earlier.

Or climbing off the couch.

Or turning off the tube.
Or getting off Facebook.
Or switching off your little handheld text machine.
Not forever.
But just for 30 to 60 minutes each day.
Regularly.
Without fail.
Because it's worth it.

Ask
Audaciously!

A Highly Underrated Strategy For Winning Big in HR – Even If You Aren't A Superstar, High-Potential Or Your Company's Next HR VP!

There are superstars in HR. And you know who I'm talking about.

These folks get chosen FIRST for the promotions.

They get picked FIRST for all of the sexy project teams and assignments.

They get the PRIORITY for exposure to the higher ups.

They are hounded, chased down and romanced by recruiters

They get the SUPREME RESPECT of their HR colleagues.

Now, don't hate them or get jealous. They deserve everything they get because they are remarkable. Their biggest challenge is sorting through all the opportunities that are dumped in their lap.

These REAL, TRUE AUTHENTIC HR superstars are in the top 1%. They are the A++ players. They are the Oprahs and Steve Jobses of HR. And everybody knows it.

A confession: I was never one of those people.

And I'll bet you're not either. The reality is very few people are. Probably only one or two exists in HR in any large organization. Some organizations don't have any. I've probably met only 5 or 6 in my entire 25 years+ in HR.

If you ARE one of those folks, then this chapter is NOT for you. Don't waste your time reading any further. Just continue doing what you're doing.

However – for the rest of us – here's my advice…

If you want more opportunities in HR, you're going to have to ASK FOR THEM.

I learned this early on in my HR career. While I was never a superstar, I was a solid performer most of the time. And every few years I was able to fall into that next quartile, somewhere in that top 25%. This was usually enough to get my foot in the door and at least compete.

But this wasn't enough by itself. Good things came when I ASKED for them.

Every significant milestone was a result of asking for it.

I contacted Quaker Oats and talked my way into one of the best HR jobs I ever had.

I volunteered for a task force that landed me my first promotion to HR manager.

I boldly asked for my next promotion and got it…18 months after I requested it.

I nominated myself for a high profile executive program.

I was once left out of an important meeting – that I attended only after practically getting on my knees and begging — that helped me build some valuable and lucrative relationships that continue to yield benefits to this day.

Those were the successes.

Now, I could fill 300 pages writing about my failures...in fact I shared a few earlier in this book. These were the times I asked and was rejected, got my feelings hurt or treated like trash. Or told "let us think about it" which over time turned into a big fat "NO." These are the real tests of your manhood (or woman-hood).

Most managers – even the great ones – aren't sitting around trying to read your mind to come up with ways to make you happy.

Now, you may be saying: hey, c'mon this ASKING thing is obvious, isn't it? And, you're right it is. But I have to tell you though, I've run into lot of people that think it's impolite, be-neath them, inappropriate, selfish, or unnecessary to have to ask for anything at work. I think some of them find it easier to stew about it and play the victim.

Here's a classic example:

Most companies have some kind of job posting system in order to make sure everybody has a shot at open positions. Now, you and both know that such programs aren't perfect, because politics are sometimes involved. But nevertheless they exist and they DO work the majority of the time.

But I've known HR people that will absolutely refuse to post for a position – even though they really want it. Their atti-tude: "They should be seeking me out for this damn job!" Then, after the position is filled, these clowns will carry a gigantic chip on their shoulder for years to come, feeling that they've been screwed over by the organization.

What a bunch of bull.

The concept of "asking" to advance your HR career doesn't just apply to job opportunities, promotions, and raises.

When was the last time you felt you should have been invit-ed to an important meeting but weren't? Did you do anything about it? The next time it happens, and you really think there's a compelling reason for you to be there, then contact the meeting leader and state your case. You may find it was just an oversight. Or, perhaps no one knew about your expertise or the role you could play. Worst case, you're told "no." So what? At least you'll know why and it shows you care.

How about upgrading your skills? Again, I've seen training budgets go unused because no one makes a request. Then, these same people will turn around and complain about a lack of development opportunities. Go figure.

Tired of that old computer or laptop in your office crashing? How about asking for a new one? I know this is a tiny, cheesy thing. But I've seen HR folks just suffer in silence and never even tell their manager, let alone ask for a replacement.

You will get more support, resources, and opportunities simply because you have the courage to ASK. In fact, the best ASKERS are often relentless – it's hard to say no to them. The rest will sit back and yell foul or favoritism, get frustrated, yet not do anything about it.

Don't fall into this trap.

In most cases, you'll have nothing to lose by asking. However, to make your "ask" work, you still have to meet at least some minimum criteria: you can't be a jerk and you must be good at what you do in HR. That's about it. If you're not, then asking will make you come across as clueless or obnoxious.

Being a good at what you do – even if you aren't a superstar — earns you the right to ask away and increases your odds of getting a "yes."

Skeptical?

Try giving it a shot.

Start with something small.

Go on just ask for it.

Now.

Steal
Shamelessly!

How Becoming A Perfectly Legal Thief
Speeds Up Your Results in HR!

We're all told that stealing is bad.

That's a lie.

Sometimes stealing can be good.

Here are four of the greatest thieves of all time...

First, there's **Steve Jobs.** Steve was shameless about swiping great ideas. In his best-selling biography by Walter Issacson, he freely admitted that Apple's monitors and their iPod were created from concepts they stole from speakers and radios produced in the 1950's and 1960's by Braun Products.

Then there's **Michael Jackson.** The self-proclaimed "King of Pop" robbed from James Brown, Jackie Wilson, The Beatles and Little Richard to create his own unique singing and dancing style starting at age 8. MJ even stole his signature dance move, "the moonwalk." from Soul Train dancers Geron Canidate and Cooley Jackson and practiced it two years before he ever performed it onstage.

Not to be outdone, there's **Kobe Bryant.** Kobe watched tapes and swiped basketball moves from Michael Jordan, Magic Johnson, Hakeem Olajuwon and Dr. J to become one of the best basketball players who ever lived.

Then there's **Pablo Picasso.** As one of the greatest artists of the 20th century, Picasso "borrowed" and "drew inspiration" from many other artists and "incorporated" them into the works of art he produced. In case you don't know what all that really means, he was a lot more blunt in the quote he's most famous for: *"Good artists copy but GREAT artists steal."*

The same behavior occurs in Human Resources.

The BEST in our profession steal.

They embrace the philosophy that you should…

Never Invent Mediocrity When You Can Steal Genius!

They've come to understand that personal growth or creating new HR initiatives from scratch always takes more time than you think and is highly overrated.

However, they don't call it stealing. They call it…

- "Benchmarking" and re-applying "best practices."
- "Modeling" someone else's behavior
- "Reverse-engineering" great HR ideas.

And all of this is perfectly legal, ethical and accepted.

In fact, the more you steal, provided that it's GOOD stealing (which I'll explain shortly), the faster you'll accelerate your success.

And that's the #1 reason why you should steal — to speed up your progress and get results quicker.

Need to improve your coaching or presentation skills? Easy. Go ask a couple of superstars you already know who do this well. Ask to observe them (they'll be flattered). Then steal their "best moves."

Want to improve your company's utilization of social media in recruiting? Simple. Visit 2-3 organizations that are already doing this better than you are. Then swipe and adapt their best practices into your organization.

Want to create a new training program to enhance the leadership skills of your managers? Don't make this overly complicated. Just take a couple of awesome programs that have already been developed. Reverse-engineer and de-construct them it to find out what makes them great. Lift the best pieces and re-apply them to your own program.

Want to create a resume or LinkedIn profile with punch and impact? Get some help. Go find 3-4 terrific examples to emulate. Analyze what they've done. Examine their word choices. See how they've packaged and presented their credentials. Scrutinize how they've laid out their skills and experiences. And then remix the best of all of these to improve your own.

Yes, it's ok.

Steal from other companies.

Swipe from other divisions within your current organization.

Lift from your role models in HR that you're inspired by, admire, like, envy and whose careers you want to follow.

That's how you will grow, develop and evolve faster in HR.

A phenomenal mentor of mine once told me a secret to his success: "In new situations, I engage in a little subtle stealing. I find the most talented person in the room, and if it's not me, I'll go stand next to him or her. I'll hang out with them. I'll observe what they say, how they behave in these situations, ask questions and try to be helpful. In situations where I find that I'm the most talented person in the room, I find another room."

While this is a form of stealing, you should recognize that there is GOOD stealing and BAD stealing.

The goal of GOOD stealing is not to plagiarize what you find, but to steal the <u>thinking</u> behind it which you can then <u>re-purpose</u> in your own style.

That's the difference between ripping off something and remixing it. Remixing requires you to take apart (reverse-engineer) the interesting idea, concept or object in order to figure out the thinking behind it as well as to identify how it works.

This knowledge helps you come up with ways to take that idea or behavior forward…adapt it…and make it work for you.

I absolutely love the simple chart below that was developed by Austin Kleon. You can find it on page 39 of his awesome little book called: **Steal Like An Artist** (StealLikeAnArtist.com). This chart shows his distinction between GOOD and BAD theft.

A GOOD thief steals from many sources, credits his sources, and then re-mixes all these influences to create something new.

A BAD thief does none of these things.

Strive to be a GOOD thief!

Have you seen something in HR worth stealing, but don't know what to do with it?

Simple.

Just create your own personal "swipe" file. Then use this file to store new ideas, best practices and stuff you've lifted from others.

Facing a tough HR dilemma? No problem. Open up that swipe file. Dig through it. You might find an answer or some inspiration there.

All of this will dramatically enhance your success in HR.

Then one day people will begin stealing from you.

And that's when you know you've arrived.

Move Sideways!

Anyone who has ever, ever won big in HR and accelerated their career has moved sideways.

What are sideways moves?

They are more commonly called **lateral moves** and most top executives in HR have built their careers by strategically accepting these kinds of assignments. They will tell you that they often had to take a sideways career step in order prepare for that next step up.

Don't believe me, then ask one of them.

So, if becoming a senior HR executive is your aspiration, you should seriously consider doing the same thing. The old-school straight-up-the-line "stovepipe" career path is a relic of the past – and frankly, it probably never existed. Today, the new-skool, hip-hop path consists of a series of zigzag moves – more of a "Z" path.

In order to become a successful global HR leader, it's important to have experience in many HR functions, geographies and business situations as possible. A "stovepipe" career path is too narrow and limited to prepare you to run a complex HR function -- especially one that is international in scope, technology-based or one that requires tapping into multiple worldwide talent communities. And most top HR jobs require experiences in all of these areas.

So, seek out lateral HR opportunities to work in different HR functions (both specialist and generalist), or across business-es (product, service, sales, manufacturing, marketing), or geographies (e.g. U.S., China, India). That's the best way to de-velop yourself as a future senior leader in HR.

However, making the RIGHT lateral move is crucial. So, in the rest of this chapter, I've laid out...

Eight Key Points To Consider Before You Decide To Move Sideways!

Be Careful During Downsizings!

At a company you love, taking a lateral move during headcount reductions obvi-ously gives you a chance to pick up a different experience and prolong your stay there.

But it's risky.

The reality is that as long company results continue to suffer, cost-cutting, belt-tightening and eliminating HR posi-tions is inevitable and likely.

You can count on it.

Most companies are impatient. Before accepting the as-signment, ask yourself how long the company results have been (or will be) spiraling downward. If it's a temporary or seasonal situation, making a lateral move can make you a much more at-tractive candidate for a promotion when business picks up.

Hopefully.

But, if the company is on its last legs without a chance of surviving, taking a lateral move may only delay the inevitable ax falling on your neck.

So, what do you do?

If you love your company and you're hell bent on staying there, take the lateral move if it's offered...AND quietly rev up your external job search <u>at</u> <u>the</u> <u>same</u> <u>time.</u> You don't want to get blindsided. Unfortunately, loyalty often works only one way.

Move Sideways Only If You're Crystal Clear On The Skills You'll Gain!

A carefully selected lateral move will give you a big bang for your buck. When it comes to developmental impact, nothing compares. Not coaching, training programs or mentoring.

In fact, you'll learn a great deal. And that's what great career management in Human Resources is all about: learning, refining and expanding your business, HR, influence and leadership skills.

There's a flip side though. A poorly chosen move can waste your time and feel duplicative. So, make sure you've pinpointed the SPECIFIC SKILLS and KEY EXPERIENCES you'll gain from the move, upfront.

Move Sideways To Expand Your Network and Marketability!

Just about ANY developmental move will expand your network, potentially improve your visibility and possibly broaden your base of support.

That's a good thing.

Working with new people and teams is especially important if you've grown tired of the people you currently work with, need a fresh challenge or simply like meeting new people.

Also, if the company later screws you, you can take your newfound skills and accomplishments and then turn yourself into a much more desirable candidate for external opportunities.

So, even if you are happy camper right now, it never hurts to "consider" a lateral move as a vehicle for enlarging your contacts and becoming a more marketable job-seeker in the future.

Take A Sideways Move To Get A Better Boss!

Your boss is critical.

But let's face it, not all of them are created equal.

Maybe it's time for you to "hire" yourself another one and show him/her what you're capable of doing.

On the other hand, your current manager might be just fine, but perhaps s/he just does not see your full potential.

Or perhaps it's time to hear a different leader's voice and learn from someone with a different perspective about HR.

The value that your new manager will provide to you is just as important as the value you'll get from the lateral assignment itself.

A great boss is your ADVOCATE and will support your success by ensuring that clear expectations are set, strong coaching and feedback are provided, barriers are removed and that your accomplishments are promoted to the higher ups.

So, if you can upgrade to a significantly better boss, a sideways move may make sense.

Don't Move Sideways If You Aren't At Least 50% Qualified For The New Role!

A key question to ask yourself is: "Is there a high probability that I'll fall flat on my face and fail in the new job?" And, "will the organization overlook my rookie mistakes if I <u>do</u> fail?"

Candidly, most organizations are not very forgiving. After six months, everybody soon forgets that this was supposed to be a "developmental assignment" for you and starts getting impatient when results don't come as quickly as envisioned.

For example, if you didn't have compensation experience and made a lateral move into the Comp & Benefits group to pick that up, it doesn't matter what you were told. After a few months, don't be surprised if you're expected to be a living, breathing comp guru.

A wise senior HR mentor once told me:

"Don't ever take a job in which you're not at least 50% qualified. No matter what they say, being perceived as 'competent' even when you're out of your element is critical to your success in HR. If you're going to win big in the new role, you'd better be a real fast learner or already bring some sort of expertise or value to the table. That can be deep knowledge about the company, a strong relationship with the clients you'll serve, good influence or leadership skills. Or something else significant! People will want to know how you can help them. They don't want to hear 'I'm here to learn.'"

So, in taking on a lateral role, immediately stress the assets you're bringing to the party. You new colleagues and clients will appreciate that and will want to help you. A credible boss who is very clear about letting people know why you're there and how you can help the team will pave the way for you too…and minimize the chance that the assignment is a failure.

Take Steps To Ensure You're Not Forgotten!

When considering a lateral move, plan for the possibility that you're "out of sight, out of mind."

I've seen this happen when people take a development move to another location – especially to a foreign country or even a U.S. location far from the main lines of the business.

You can simply fall off the radar screen. It's especially risky if the person that put you in this job leaves the company. It can feel like you're stranded in a foreign country without a passport.

To minimize this, here are a couple of recommendations:

#1: Create your own "Board of Directors." This group is made up of your sponsors, mentors and advocates...in addition to your boss. Keep the communications lines open with ALL of them. Provide them with regular updates on how you're doing and get brutally candid feedback. This can be one of the most powerful ways to ensure that you're not abandoned in a lateral move. It's even more crucial in geographic moves, where you can become isolated from your established network and far removed from the watchful eyes of corporate headquarters.

#2: Request a "lifeline." No, not the one on *Who Wants To Be A Millionaire*. The lifeline we're talking about is an informal or formal (written) agreement that if things don't work out, you can return to your old position or an equivalent one. Many companies will tell you: "That's crazy, we don't do that!" Or they'll say: "What's up with that, that's pathetic, don't you have confidence in yourself?" Don't let these putdowns or the fear your company may say "NO," keep you from at least asking about a lifeline. You are merely doing good career due diligence and creating a contingency plan for yourself in today's volatile business climate where anything can happen. Sure, it's a long shot. But at a minimum, have it on your list and put it on the table for discussion before accepting the job. It doesn't hurt to ask, especially if this is a high risk move.

Know How Long Is Enough!

What's the answer to the question of: "How long should you spent in a lateral assignment?"

The answer is: It should be long enough to learn and make a significant contribution. Generally, in year one, you learn and in year two, you make your impact. Then it's time to move on.

If your stay in the assignment is too short (less than 18 months) there isn't enough time to have an impact. If your stay in the role is too long, the payoff diminishes and you can feel plateaued or abandoned. Obviously there are exceptions. If you're early in your HR career, the assignment may not need to be as long. Complicated HR leadership roles with enormous amounts of scope, scale and responsibilities may require more than two years.

In most cases however, 18 to 24 months as a good, general rule of thumb for staying in a lateral assignment.

Some Final Thoughts...

No matter what I've said so far. Let me be perfectly clear: lateral moves are not for everyone. If your aspiration is to win big as a specialist in HR – whether that's compensation, talent acquisition or labor relations – it may not be your cup of tea. I'm all for staying put as long as you continue to be happy and marketable.

However, be aware of the potential benefits and risks to your HR career, and make the decision that's right for you. Don't let anyone (like me) talk you into doing something that you don't want to do or is not in your best interest.

Also, if you're contemplating a sideways move, talk it over with your current boss. If you have mentors, schedule a meeting with them too. Take them through the information in this chapter. Get their input.

Making lateral moves at key junctures in your HR career will build your career and help you win big in the long run. But before you making that leap, be sure to ask yourself some tough questions, talk to some trusted advisers, do your research and make an informed decision.

Put Up The Mirror...Often!

I was devastated the first time I received 360 feedback from my HR team.

This occurred when I was promoted into my very first HR manager position.

In this new leadership role, I had three direct reports and our HR team supported the foods manufacturing function for Quaker Oats.

As a young guy early in my HR career, I had fantasized about making it to the big time and becoming a huge success in HR. As part of my dream, I thought about how great it would be to run my own HR function, have my own team and call the shots.

I had now taken a key first step towards realizing that long-awaited aspiration.

I also knew that going through the company-mandated 360 process was an important part of my development. It would give me a chance to "put up a mirror" and see myself from the perspective of my team. And, deep down inside, I was curious about how they *really* felt about me.

However, I soon found out that...

One of the biggest hurdles you face in getting the maximum value from personal feedback is YOUR OWN EGO.

This realization hit me head on when I got my 360 results back. As I opened the green envelope containing my feedback, I was a little nervous, but confident that I was going to be pleased. After all, even though I was a brand new HR manager, I wasn't new to HR. In my prior HR roles, I had trained literally hundreds of managers on how to coach, handle conflicts, build teams and get the most from their direct reports.

Not to be cocky, but I felt I was an expert on how to manage people.

As I now read through my results…

It became clear that it didn't matter how I felt. My direct reports did NOT regard me as a good manager. Not even close. In their feedback, they all let me have it! Nothing was sugarcoated. Nothing was held back. All their guns were blazing!

According to their feedback:

- *They didn't feel that I was committed to them, their performance or their careers.*
- *I was too hands off and distant. They didn't believe I provided enough direction and was too dependent on them to work out their own problems and issues on their own.*
- *I was too blue sky and not detailed enough. They wanted more clarification and details on projects and more face time with me when they encountered problems*
- *Most felt that I had impossibly high standards and as a result I was quick on the trigger with criticism and blame. Even when they hustled, busted their butt, and delivered the goods, they felt I was much, much too slow to give them atta-boy's, recognition and acknowledgment.*
- *And finally, to them, I seemed much more concerned about my own career than furthering theirs.*

Wow!

Ouch!

After reading all this, I was stunned.

At first, I thought their comments were grossly unfair. I felt I had bent over backwards to be a great manager and was thoroughly shocked they didn't feel the same way.

I spent the next few days pissed off at my team and walked around in a sour mood. I'm sure they picked up my negative vibe, but no one said a word. After a few days of stewing over these results and talking with a couple of my mentors about it, I decided to swallow my ego and do what I'd coached managers to do in similar situations, which was....

To take action by sitting down and talking with my team directly about the brutally candid feedback they had provided me.

However, even though I wanted to talk, they didn't.

They could tell I was angry. No one was anxious to come to a meeting and get chewed out. I had to calm down and pledge to them that there would be no butt kickings and that I was not out to destroy their careers. I candidly admitted to them that yes, while I was stung by some of their feedback, I needed to understand it better in order to make the personal improvements they wanted me to make as their leader and to enhance the working relationship within our team. And that none of this could occur without their help in clarifying their feedback.

Thankfully (for me), they bravely agreed to meet and provide me with the information I asked for. In our meeting, they didn't hold back. While I held my tongue, they were very specific, gave me great examples and offered excellent suggestions for improvement. They opened my eyes to blind spots in my leadership style that I didn't know I had and which had held our team back.

I thanked them for their courage and candor. I made a commitment right then and there to act on their feedback. And, in the ensuing months, I worked hard to adjust my leadership style based on their feedback and had many follow up discussions with them to check how I was progressing in their eyes. It took me two years to work through these issues and to finally find my stride as a new HR manager.

From that first experience getting my 360 results as a new HR leader, I re-learned an obvious, but valuable lesson…

HOLD UP THE MIRROR – REGULARLY
by embracing the power of candid feedback.

Get feedback from your boss, your clients and your team.

Don't shortchange this as a tool for improving your effectiveness as an HR professional.

However, be prepared. Don't be surprised if the feedback you get is unclear, doesn't make sense or even seems unfair. Very few people or organizations give feedback clearly. It is often vague and confusing – sometimes intentionally so – because it's uncomfortable to provide it and no one wants to chase away "solid" performers.

So, it's up to you to get beyond the labels and cryptic statements – to dig out the REAL concerns about how you're viewed in the organization.

But don't let these hurdles deter you.

A major factor in enhancing your HR career is continually seeking out this kind of information.

And then ACTING aggressively on it.

Stay On Top
Of Your Game!

Ever get to a point in your HR job where you're just...dog tired and worn out?

Here's what I mean...

You need a forklift to pull yourself out of bed every morning.

Your clients are bugging the living crap out of you.

That HR assignment that you went after like a killer whale...now feels like a chore.

Those tedious little admin tasks that are a part of every single HR job ever invented, are now getting on your last nerve.

You don't want to quit, but you need to get some of your old mojo back.

What happened to the way things were when you first started out?

Well, HR jobs are just like marriages. Sometimes you've got to put in a little extra effort to keep that ol' spark alive.

The same techniques that can rekindle the spark with your significant other can be used to keep the candle lit at work too.

To that end, here are…

7 Ways To Fall Back In Love With HR All Over Again! (And Maintain Your Edge)

Learn Something New!

Your brain was not meant to soak up all the knowledge it needed by age 22, and then shut down.

As soon as you quit learning and growing, you start to die. If you think about it, that's what made HR work so much fun in the first place — that ridiculously crazy learning curve you were on. At times, you may have felt like you were drinking from a fire hydrant, but it was also a thrill.

It's critical to your HR career (and your self-respect) that you keep learning. As soon as you begin to get too comfortable, resting on what you already know, you'll also start to get stale. And before you know it, some devious, arrogant little prick disguised as a one of your colleagues will show up and start kicking your butt intellectually and with new ideas…in meetings, with your clients and in front of your boss.

What do you do to ward this off?

Add a new skill to your bag of tricks. Or get even more amazing at some of the skills you already possess. Dive into a topic that scares you, like deepening your knowledge of your company's business. Or becoming better at developing talent. Or engaging employees. Or using social media in HR. Or exploring whatever the wild frontiers are in your HR specialty area.

You don't have study like you're trying to pass the SPHR certification exam. But make sure you're being challenged in picking up this new know-how. Learning something new will give you a nice refreshing dip back in the deep end of the pool where the big fish swim.

Get Thee To A Seminar!

If your problem is self-doubt, imposter syndrome, or believing you're not delivering enough value, get over it. And then sneak out to a 2-3 day seminar.

Nope, NOT a webinar. Physically get out of the office. Even if you're an introvert, you'll profit from the face-to-face, full-frontal interaction with different people.

When you get there, totally disconnect! Keep the texting and e-mails at an absolute minimum. Yeah, I know it's tough. But just concentrate on getting energized by new people with new ideas in a new setting.

Great seminars are the fastest way I know to re-charge dead batteries. It's also amazing to see firsthand how much you will get jazzed up by being out of the office and invigorated by new external perspectives. And that's the kind of joyful feeling that lasts longer a pint of Ben & Jerry's.

Re-Connect!

Quick, identify the five people who have influenced your HR career the most.

Today, take ONE of them to lunch. Or call one of them and talk for an hour. Then, make plans to re-connect with the other four in the next week.

Remember how they used to inspire you.

Well, let them pump you up all over again.

Re-connect with that boss that gave you your first big break in HR. You know, the one you and everyone else admired. The one who was patient and supportive as you were learning the ropes.

Re-connect with the former client that taught you ten times more about the business than you ever taught them about HR.

Re-connect with the colleague that you hit it off with on day one, who always had a great take on the world and who always made you laugh.

Re-connect with them and let the magic happen...again.

Write Your HR Career Manifesto!

One of the best companies in the world at engaging employees is Zappo's.

What makes them great is that early on Tony Hsieh, their CEO, and his team sat down and figured out what the business stood for -- their core values.

They grabbed a piece of paper, found a room, put their heads together and decided who they wanted to be...and who they *didn't* want to be.

The same thing applies to your career.

Come up with 10 important core values you stand for. If they don't make you tingle, you're not being honest.

But do me a favor.

Don't put down boring HR buzzwords like being a "strategic business partner." (Refer to #9, page 10).

Dig deep into your soul.

Find some values that put a lump in your throat.

Now, think about how you're going to live your new statement of values this week.

What are you going to do to show your organization, your boss, your colleagues, your dog and the rest of the world that you stand for?

Leverage Your Towering Strengths!

The two biggest mistakes that I see folks in HR make is:

- Wasting time trying to improve their weaknesses
- Not spending enough time building on their strengths

Years of research by Martin Seligman (AuthenticHappiness.com), Donald Clifton (StrengthsFinder 2.0) and others have conclusively proven that people have much more success and enjoyment at work when they've identified what they're good at and then spend time doing it on the job.

Do you know what your strengths are? If not, there are lots of assessment tools that can tell you. Personally, I like Myers-Briggs. A friend of mine swears by Strengths Finder 2.0. You can also get at your gifts by simply asking ten people who know you well what you excel at.

However, don't waste time sweating these options. The approach you use is less important than digging out the personal attributes that you've been particularly blessed with...and then deciding how you're going to deploy at least one of them more on the job.

Perhaps you love taking things from good to great (this is the "Maximizer" strength in StrengthsFinder 2.0). If so, on the job, you'll want to look at taking on more "improvement projects" versus just doing HR work that just maintains the status quo. Or maybe your strength is "Empathy" which means you'll quickly get bored if you can't occasionally spice up your work with some employee relations and coaching work.

Using your signature strengths more on the job is a blast. And, they'll help you endure the rough spots that are inevitable when you deal with cranky personalities all day long in Human Resources.

And if you keep looking for fresh ways to apply your strengths to your work, your love of that work will rarely grow old.

Get a Mentor or Coach!

Some HR folks can be foolish and short-sighted. And candidly, I'm in this group. We think we can do everything alone. While we don't hesitate to engage mentors and coaches to work with our clients, we rarely use them ourselves. We become addicted to drawing our own map.

And that's all well and good. You need to be self-reliant. But no one will accuse you of cheating if you go get some help, as well.

When I first became an HR leader, I wasn't very good. I had a lot of passion, know-how and drive, but there were definitely many days where I could have been sued for managerial malpractice. But fortunately for me, my HR team let me know it by hammering me in my first 360 feedback session with them…to their credit.

With ego bruised, and my boss' support, I started working with a coach. Not just a good coach, a great one. One who had been there and done that. He injected me with confidence, helped shave off my rough edges and helped me do what I needed to do as a manager. He also helped me enjoy the process of leading an HR team a whole lot more.

Just like a personal trainer at the gym, a great coach won't do the work for you. But they *can* help energize you and realize that you're strong enough to do the work yourself.

I still have lunch with my coach a couple of times a year. Though we each have gone in different directions and haven't formerly worked together in years, the relationship remains. And, it is one that I'll cherish forever.

In selecting a coach, the important thing is that you find someone who clicks with you, shares your values, and has a style that will challenge and push you to do more than you can do alone.

Schedule Time Away From Your HR Day Job!

I don't want to leave this one out because this can be the most effective approach of all.

But, it's the toughest to pull off.

Here's the deal: I don't care how much you love your job. I don't care how much energy it gives you. If it's your calling, give it all the juice and passion you have to offer...**then you've got to step away.**

When you create a career and start to live your dream, it's easy to think you should do that 24/7, 365.

But that's a quick path to burnout.

You'll be more creative, more stimulated, and more excited about your career when you carve out time to do some of that *other* stuff you love.

You don't have to run a marathon if that isn't your thing. But get out for a walk, jog or a bike ride every day. It improves your mental clarity, your mood, and cuts your risk of pretty much every kind of disease. You'll be a lot more productive, too, which is a nice bonus.

But don't stop there.

Schedule some time to just play. Go to the movies. Take some photos and wacky shots to laugh about and share with others. Draw, finger paint or read some comic books. Just do something you find relaxing and fun. Don't make it too practical. If it has any redeeming social value whatsoever, it doesn't count. Give that inner four-year-old some play time, and watch what that does for the rest of your life.

There you are. Seven actions you can take to keep your batteries charged, reclaim your love of HR...and keep you on top of your game.

Lastly,
Leave A Legacy!

The Final Piece of Winning Big In HR

There's nothing wrong with getting insanely great results in HR and having your clients rave about you as an HR professional.

And the 100+ strategies, stories and advice that I've provided in the previous chapters should have given you a few ideas on how to accomplish just that.

However, I'd like to leave you with one final piece of the puzzle and it is this: **If you want to truly win BIG in HR in the long-term, you must involve yourself in serving a much BIGGER and HIGHER purpose in HR beyond just your own personal success.** And I believe you can only do this by finding time to…

Make an impact in the lives of other people!

Yes, I know I've mentioned this more than a couple of other times throughout this book, but I want to wrap this book up by driving this point home because it's that important.

Don't misunderstand. I am not suggesting that you should minimize the pursuit of doing great HR work, achieving career success, building wealth and helping your organization succeed.

Not at all.

However, I am encouraging you to use the terrific platform you have as an HR professional to also <u>LEAVE</u> <u>A</u> <u>LEGACY</u> as a person who made a difference.

Life is short.

Your HR career is even shorter.

You never know when either might end.

You see, I don't think of HR as a job. Or even as a career. And it's certainly not as something that is owned by the company you happen to work for at the moment. I regard HR as a *calling*.

A calling because I deeply believe part of our life's purpose is to make a difference and lend a hand to those who are trying to live life productively and get ahead.

Chances are someone extended a hand at various points to help you through your HR career. And if so, I believe you have an obligation let others benefit from your wisdom and experience. For example:

- If you've struggled through setbacks in your job or career...and you've survived and learned from it, you should help those now struggling by sharing your lessons.
- If you've achieved the impossible, you should take some time and share the insights you've gained to make it possible for others to achieve the same.
- If you've spent years in HR figuring something out, why not shorten someone else's learning curve?
- If you have cracked to code to success in any area within HR field, why not let others in on your secrets?

All of this involves coming from a place of wanting to SERVE others by sharing your know-how to INSPIRE and INSTRUCT them in areas you've mastered or take for granted.

And it's the best HR legacy you can ever leave because it will always exist in the hearts, minds and memories of those you've helped long beyond the time your career in HR has concluded.

The key in making this type of change is to change your focus from the word "ME" to the word "YOU" and set aside time to accomplish some YOU-focused activities directed at benefiting others.

This simple shift in your mindset and focus can singlehandedly turn around your HR career all by itself and give you unbelievable levels of personal fulfillment.

But you must build time into your calendar and look for ways to put your needs second to those of your team, your boss, your clients or others that you care about.

This could include specific things like:

- Volunteering to coach or mentor those with less HR experience.
- Taking time to personally step in and help onboard new people in your organization who are scared and feel abandoned in their first few weeks on the job.
- Putting yourself in someone's life as a sounding board when they are struggling to succeed on the job.
- Starting an employee recognition program that acknowledges those who are doing a great job, but are going unappreciated for their efforts. Administrative assistants, technicians or other back office employees are great examples of those doing terrific work that goes unnoticed.
- Letting a high school student or college intern "shadow" you for a day to observe you on the job.
- Sharing your HR story or experience on campuses, at Career Days and with HR associations.
- Introducing people in your network to others or helping to connect people together.
- Sharing your HR experiences in a book, blog, white paper or posting it online for the entire world of HR to benefit from. (If you're interested in these activities, you'll want to check out my book: Your HR Goldmine.)
- Volunteering your time at your local Boys and Girls Club.

- Contributing your time to advancing causes that you are passionate about.

Helping other people and organizations is the heart of the HR profession. You, like me, were probably drawn to the field for this reason. And, as an HR you have a natural platform to assist, enable and support others in their pursuit of success.

Take advantage of it.

Personally, I only began experiencing success in HR in a _truly meaningful way_ when I started stepping up my efforts to be of more service to others. I consider my best HR work to be: (1) the scholarship program that I started years ago in memory of my son who died in a tragic car accident and (2) sharing my own personal HR experiences with other professionals through my blog, books, speaking and consulting. These activities have been far more fulfilling to me than anything that I've ever accomplished as an HR executive.

And it is my hope that if I'm remembered ONLY for these two things, then I will have won BIG in HR – and I will have been pleased with my legacy as an HR professional.

And the same legacy opportunity exists for you if you choose to embrace this last piece of the puzzle!

By taking time to give back and making special efforts to put others' interests first, you'll find that your manager, your clients and your colleagues will follow you, support you, give you the benefit of the doubt…and embrace your ideas faster, eagerly and more readily.

And opportunities will emerge that you will not have envisioned or anticipated.

I'm certain of it.

And that, my friend, is what winning big in HR is all about.

Onward!

CONNECT TO US ONLINE!
DISCOVER MORE WAYS TO SUCCEED IN HUMAN RESOUCES

Follow us on Twitter:
@SuccessInHR

Subscribe to our Blog:
SuccessInHR.com

"Like" us on Facebook:
Facebook.com/SuccessInHRDaily

Connect with us on LinkedIn:
http://LinkedIn.com/SuccessInHR

THE BRYAN A. COLLINS
SCHOLARSHIP PROGRAM

 The Bryan A. Collins Memorial Scholarship Program awards scholarship grants every year to minority students who demonstrate excellence in pursuit of their college degrees. Students selected for this scholarship must embody the values embraced by the late Bryan A. Collins -- great with people, great at academics and great in extra-curricular leadership activities.

Bryan Collins was a rising star and well-respected student leader at Tennessee State University. Bryan received his B.S. degree in Biology from TSU in May 2005. At the time of his passing, he was enrolled in the Masters program in physical therapy and anxiously looking forward to commencing his doctoral studies. On campus, he was a leader in the Kappa Alpha Psi fraternity, served on the Civic Committee, the Community Service Committee and help set strategic direction as a Board Member of the fraternity.

In addition, he found much success outside the classroom. He was voted Mr. Tennessee State first runner-up, was involved in the Student Union Board of Governors, was a founding member of the Generation of Educated Men and worked closely with the Tennessee State University dean of admissions and records.

Bryan found comfort and relaxation in sports, music, movies, video games, friends, good parties and just spending time with his family relaxing at home.

The key contributors to Bryan's scholarship program include the PepsiCo Foundation, Pamela Hewitt & Warren Lawson of Chicago, the Motorola Foundation and many other organizations and individuals. Additional details about Bryan, the scholarship program and how to contribute can be found at the scholarship website at: www.BryanCollinsScholarship.org.

ABOUT THE AUTHOR

Alan Collins is **Founder of Success in HR**, a company dedicated to empowering HR professionals and executives around the globe with insights and tools for enhancing their careers.

He was formerly Vice President of Human Resources at PepsiCo where he led HR initiatives for their North American Quaker Oats, Gatorade and Tropicana businesses.

With 25 years as an HR executive and professional, Alan's corporate and operating human resources experience is extensive. He led an organization of 60 HR directors, managers and professionals spread across 21 different locations in North America, where he was accountable for their performance, careers and success. He and his team provided HR strategic and executional oversight for a workforce of over 7000 employees supporting $8 billion in sales. Alan also served as the HR M&A lead in integrating new acquisitions as well as divesting existing businesses; and he provided HR leadership for one of the largest change initiatives in the history of the Pepsi organization.

As the co-leader of the Quaker Tropicana Gatorade African American Network, Alan was selected as a member of the prestigious Executive Leadership Council, based in Washington D.C. He has also taught at various Chicago-area universities.

Alan is author of numerous books on Human Resources – including the HR best sellers *Unwritten HR Rules* and *Best Kept HR Secrets*. Both have been ranked among Amazon's top 10 books for HR professionals. In addition, he has written over 100 articles and white papers on HR that have appeared in *HR Executive Magazine, HRM Today* and other nationally-known publications for human resources professionals.

He received his BS and MS degrees in Industrial Relations from Purdue. More about Alan and his works can be accessed at: www.SuccessInHR.com.

Made in the USA
Coppell, TX
04 February 2020